A YEAR OF WEEKLY BAKING BY:

_____

BREAD JOURNAL

A Year of Weekly Baking

CHRONICLE BOOKS

SAN FRANCISCO

Library of Congress Cataloging-
in-Publication Data available.

ISBN 978-1-4521-0872-8

Manufactured in China

10 9 8 7 6 5 4 3 2 1

Chronicle Books LLC
680 Second Street
San Francisco, California 94107
www.chroniclebooks.com

HOW TO USE THIS JOURNAL

You have pledged to build your bread-baking practice. You have the iron-clad commitment, gathered the ingredients to experiment with, and carved out a slice of time once or twice a week to dedicate to mastering the art of baking bread. But, how do you record and improve your bread-baking skills?

A bread journal can help immensely. This book will chart your progress over the course of a year, of baking bread twice a week. Use these charts first as inspiration, then as record of the ingredients you choose as well as the conditions that factor into your loaves: timing, temperature. Record your taste and visual impressions. When your bread is flawed, troubleshoot using all of the data you've recorded.

At the end of a year of bread baking, look back over what you have accomplished, at this journal—your scientific record of building the perfect loaf.

INGREDIENTS

TYPES OF FLOUR

- ☐ ALL-PURPOSE
- ☐ UNBLEACHED ALL-PURPOSE
- ☐ BREAD FLOUR
- ☐ UNBLEACHED WHEAT
  - ___ *Plus malted*
  - ___ *Low ash*
  - ___ *Malted All-purpose*
  - ___ *High-gluten*
- ☐ WHOLE-WHEAT
  - ___ *Fine*
  - ___ *High-protein fine*
  - ___ *Medium*
  - ___ *High-protein medium*
  - ___ *Coarse*
  - ___ *High-protein coarse*
  - ___ *Special medium/coarse*

- ☐ HARD WHITE WHOLE-WHEAT
- ☐ BROMATED HIGH-PROTEIN
- ☐ UNBLEACHED ENRICHED
- ☐ BLEACHED WHEAT
- ☐ ARTISAN BREAD
- ☐ IRISH-STYLE WHOLEMEAL
- ☐ HIGH-GLUTEN
- ☐ HIGH-EXTRACTION
  - ___ *Type 70 malted*
  - ___ *Stone ground type 80*
  - ___ *Type 80*
  - ___ *Old country type 85*
  - ___ *Old country type 85 malted*
- ☐ OTHER _____

- ☐ SPECIALTY
  - ___ *Barley*
  - ___ *Coarse cornmeal*
  - ___ *Fine cornmeal*
  - ___ *Polenta*
  - ___ *Flaxseed meal*
  - ___ *Millet*
  - ___ *Brown rice*
  - ___ *White rice*
  - ___ *Cream of rye*
  - ___ *Pumpernickel rye*
  - ___ *White rye*
  - ___ *Whole dark rye*
  - ___ *Spelt*
  - ___ *Semolina*
  - ___ *Whole durum*
  - ___ *Whole-wheat durum*

TYPES OF SALT

- ☐ IODIZED TABLE SALT
- ☐ KOSHER MEDIUM-COARSE SALT
- ☐ PINK HIMALAYAN SALT
- ☐ VOLCANIC BLACK SALT
- ☐ MALDON SALT
- ☐ EXTRA FINE SEA SALT
- ☐ FRENCH GRAY SEA SALT
- ☐ SMOKED SEA SALT
- ☐ SEL GRIS

BAKING CONDITIONS

HUMIDITY

TEMPERATURE

STARTER DESCRIPTION

FINISHED LOAF DESCRIPTION

CRUMB DESCRIPTORS

- ☐ EVEN, "TIGHT" HOLES
- ☐ EVEN, MEDIUM HOLES
- ☐ IRREGULAR, LARGE HOLES
- ☐ DELICATE STRUCTURE
- ☐ AVERAGE STRUCTURE
- ☐ STURDY STRUCTURE
- ☐ TRANSLUCENT
- ☐ DENSE
- ☐ COOL AND CREAMY
- ☐ DRY OR DUSTY
- ☐ OTHER _____

CRUST DESCRIPTORS

- ☐ TENDER, GOLDEN
- ☐ SOFT, COMPRESSIBLE
- ☐ HARD, CRUSTY
- ☐ CARAMELIZED
- ☐ NUTTY
- ☐ BUTTERY
- ☐ OILY
- ☐ TOOTHSOME
- ☐ CRISPY
- ☐ OTHER _____

DATE _____

NOTES

INGREDIENTS

TYPES OF FLOUR

- ☐ ALL-PURPOSE
- ☐ UNBLEACHED ALL-PURPOSE
- ☐ BREAD FLOUR
- ☐ UNBLEACHED WHEAT
  - ___ *Plus malted*
  - ___ *Low ash*
  - ___ *Malted All-purpose*
  - ___ *High-gluten*
- ☐ WHOLE-WHEAT
  - ___ *Fine*
  - ___ *High-protein fine*
  - ___ *Medium*
  - ___ *High-protein medium*
  - ___ *Coarse*
  - ___ *High-protein coarse*
  - ___ *Special medium/coarse*

- ☐ HARD WHITE WHOLE-WHEAT
- ☐ BROMATED HIGH-PROTEIN
- ☐ UNBLEACHED ENRICHED
- ☐ BLEACHED WHEAT
- ☐ ARTISAN BREAD
- ☐ IRISH-STYLE WHOLEMEAL
- ☐ HIGH-GLUTEN
- ☐ HIGH-EXTRACTION
  - ___ *Type 70 malted*
  - ___ *Stone ground type 80*
  - ___ *Type 80*
  - ___ *Old country type 85*
  - ___ *Old country type 85 malted*
- ☐ OTHER _____

- ☐ SPECIALTY
  - ___ *Barley*
  - ___ *Coarse cornmeal*
  - ___ *Fine cornmeal*
  - ___ *Polenta*
  - ___ *Flaxseed meal*
  - ___ *Millet*
  - ___ *Brown rice*
  - ___ *White rice*
  - ___ *Cream of rye*
  - ___ *Pumpernickel rye*
  - ___ *White rye*
  - ___ *Whole dark rye*
  - ___ *Spelt*
  - ___ *Semolina*
  - ___ *Whole durum*
  - ___ *Whole-wheat durum*

TYPES OF SALT

- ☐ IODIZED TABLE SALT
- ☐ KOSHER MEDIUM-COARSE SALT
- ☐ PINK HIMALAYAN SALT
- ☐ VOLCANIC BLACK SALT
- ☐ MALDON SALT
- ☐ EXTRA FINE SEA SALT
- ☐ FRENCH GRAY SEA SALT
- ☐ SMOKED SEA SALT
- ☐ SEL GRIS

BAKING CONDITIONS

HUMIDITY

TEMPERATURE

STARTER DESCRIPTION

FINISHED LOAF DESCRIPTION

CRUMB DESCRIPTORS

- ☐ EVEN, "TIGHT" HOLES
- ☐ EVEN, MEDIUM HOLES
- ☐ IRREGULAR, LARGE HOLES
- ☐ DELICATE STRUCTURE
- ☐ AVERAGE STRUCTURE
- ☐ STURDY STRUCTURE
- ☐ TRANSLUCENT
- ☐ DENSE
- ☐ COOL AND CREAMY
- ☐ DRY OR DUSTY
- ☐ OTHER _____

CRUST DESCRIPTORS

- ☐ TENDER, GOLDEN
- ☐ SOFT, COMPRESSIBLE
- ☐ HARD, CRUSTY
- ☐ CARAMELIZED
- ☐ NUTTY
- ☐ BUTTERY
- ☐ OILY
- ☐ TOOTHSOME
- ☐ CRISPY
- ☐ OTHER _____

DATE _____

INGREDIENTS

TYPES OF FLOUR

- [ ] ALL-PURPOSE
- [ ] UNBLEACHED ALL-PURPOSE
- [ ] BREAD FLOUR
- [ ] UNBLEACHED WHEAT
  - ___ *Plus malted*
  - ___ *Low ash*
  - ___ *Malted All-purpose*
  - ___ *High-gluten*
- [ ] WHOLE-WHEAT
  - ___ *Fine*
  - ___ *High-protein fine*
  - ___ *Medium*
  - ___ *High-protein medium*
  - ___ *Coarse*
  - ___ *High-protein coarse*
  - ___ *Special medium/coarse*

- [ ] HARD WHITE WHOLE-WHEAT
- [ ] BROMATED HIGH-PROTEIN
- [ ] UNBLEACHED ENRICHED
- [ ] BLEACHED WHEAT
- [ ] ARTISAN BREAD
- [ ] IRISH-STYLE WHOLEMEAL
- [ ] HIGH-GLUTEN
- [ ] HIGH-EXTRACTION
  - ___ *Type 70 malted*
  - ___ *Stone ground type 80*
  - ___ *Type 80*
  - ___ *Old country type 85*
  - ___ *Old country type 85 malted*
- [ ] OTHER _____

- [ ] SPECIALTY
  - ___ *Barley*
  - ___ *Coarse cornmeal*
  - ___ *Fine cornmeal*
  - ___ *Polenta*
  - ___ *Flaxseed meal*
  - ___ *Millet*
  - ___ *Brown rice*
  - ___ *White rice*
  - ___ *Cream of rye*
  - ___ *Pumpernickel rye*
  - ___ *White rye*
  - ___ *Whole dark rye*
  - ___ *Spelt*
  - ___ *Semolina*
  - ___ *Whole durum*
  - ___ *Whole-wheat durum*

TYPES OF SALT

- [ ] IODIZED TABLE SALT
- [ ] KOSHER MEDIUM-COARSE SALT
- [ ] PINK HIMALAYAN SALT
- [ ] VOLCANIC BLACK SALT
- [ ] MALDON SALT
- [ ] EXTRA FINE SEA SALT
- [ ] FRENCH GRAY SEA SALT
- [ ] SMOKED SEA SALT
- [ ] SEL GRIS

BAKING CONDITIONS

HUMIDITY

TEMPERATURE

STARTER DESCRIPTION

FINISHED LOAF DESCRIPTION

CRUMB DESCRIPTORS

- [ ] EVEN, "TIGHT" HOLES
- [ ] EVEN, MEDIUM HOLES
- [ ] IRREGULAR, LARGE HOLES
- [ ] DELICATE STRUCTURE
- [ ] AVERAGE STRUCTURE
- [ ] STURDY STRUCTURE
- [ ] TRANSLUCENT
- [ ] DENSE
- [ ] COOL AND CREAMY
- [ ] DRY OR DUSTY
- [ ] OTHER _____

CRUST DESCRIPTORS

- [ ] TENDER, GOLDEN
- [ ] SOFT, COMPRESSIBLE
- [ ] HARD, CRUSTY
- [ ] CARAMELIZED
- [ ] NUTTY
- [ ] BUTTERY
- [ ] OILY
- [ ] TOOTHSOME
- [ ] CRISPY
- [ ] OTHER _____

DATE _____

NOTES

INGREDIENTS

TYPES OF FLOUR

☐ ALL-PURPOSE
☐ UNBLEACHED ALL-PURPOSE
☐ BREAD FLOUR
☐ UNBLEACHED WHEAT
___ *Plus malted*
___ *Low ash*
___ *Malted All-purpose*
___ *High-gluten*
☐ WHOLE-WHEAT
___ *Fine*
___ *High-protein fine*
___ *Medium*
___ *High-protein medium*
___ *Coarse*
___ *High-protein coarse*
___ *Special medium/coarse*

☐ HARD WHITE WHOLE-WHEAT
☐ BROMATED HIGH-PROTEIN
☐ UNBLEACHED ENRICHED
☐ BLEACHED WHEAT
☐ ARTISAN BREAD
☐ IRISH-STYLE WHOLEMEAL
☐ HIGH-GLUTEN
☐ HIGH-EXTRACTION
___ *Type 70 malted*
___ *Stone ground type 80*
___ *Type 80*
___ *Old country type 85*
___ *Old country type 85 malted*
☐ OTHER _____

☐ SPECIALTY
___ *Barley*
___ *Coarse cornmeal*
___ *Fine cornmeal*
___ *Polenta*
___ *Flaxseed meal*
___ *Millet*
___ *Brown rice*
___ *White rice*
___ *Cream of rye*
___ *Pumpernickel rye*
___ *White rye*
___ *Whole dark rye*
___ *Spelt*
___ *Semolina*
___ *Whole durum*
___ *Whole-wheat durum*

TYPES OF SALT

☐ IODIZED TABLE SALT
☐ KOSHER MEDIUM-COARSE SALT
☐ PINK HIMALAYAN SALT
☐ VOLCANIC BLACK SALT
☐ MALDON SALT
☐ EXTRA FINE SEA SALT
☐ FRENCH GRAY SEA SALT
☐ SMOKED SEA SALT
☐ SEL GRIS

BAKING CONDITIONS

HUMIDITY

TEMPERATURE

STARTER DESCRIPTION

FINISHED LOAF DESCRIPTION

CRUMB DESCRIPTORS

☐ EVEN, "TIGHT" HOLES
☐ EVEN, MEDIUM HOLES
☐ IRREGULAR, LARGE HOLES
☐ DELICATE STRUCTURE
☐ AVERAGE STRUCTURE
☐ STURDY STRUCTURE
☐ TRANSLUCENT
☐ DENSE
☐ COOL AND CREAMY
☐ DRY OR DUSTY
☐ OTHER _____

CRUST DESCRIPTORS

☐ TENDER, GOLDEN
☐ SOFT, COMPRESSIBLE
☐ HARD, CRUSTY
☐ CARAMELIZED
☐ NUTTY
☐ BUTTERY
☐ OILY
☐ TOOTHSOME
☐ CRISPY
☐ OTHER _____

DATE _____

NOTES

INGREDIENTS

TYPES OF FLOUR

- ☐ ALL-PURPOSE
- ☐ UNBLEACHED ALL-PURPOSE
- ☐ BREAD FLOUR
- ☐ UNBLEACHED WHEAT
  - ___ *Plus malted*
  - ___ *Low ash*
  - ___ *Malted All-purpose*
  - ___ *High-gluten*
- ☐ WHOLE-WHEAT
  - ___ *Fine*
  - ___ *High-protein fine*
  - ___ *Medium*
  - ___ *High-protein medium*
  - ___ *Coarse*
  - ___ *High-protein coarse*
  - ___ *Special medium/coarse*

- ☐ HARD WHITE WHOLE-WHEAT
- ☐ BROMATED HIGH-PROTEIN
- ☐ UNBLEACHED ENRICHED
- ☐ BLEACHED WHEAT
- ☐ ARTISAN BREAD
- ☐ IRISH-STYLE WHOLEMEAL
- ☐ HIGH-GLUTEN
- ☐ HIGH-EXTRACTION
  - ___ *Type 70 malted*
  - ___ *Stone ground type 80*
  - ___ *Type 80*
  - ___ *Old country type 85*
  - ___ *Old country type 85 malted*
- ☐ OTHER _____

- ☐ SPECIALTY
  - ___ *Barley*
  - ___ *Coarse cornmeal*
  - ___ *Fine cornmeal*
  - ___ *Polenta*
  - ___ *Flaxseed meal*
  - ___ *Millet*
  - ___ *Brown rice*
  - ___ *White rice*
  - ___ *Cream of rye*
  - ___ *Pumpernickel rye*
  - ___ *White rye*
  - ___ *Whole dark rye*
  - ___ *Spelt*
  - ___ *Semolina*
  - ___ *Whole durum*
  - ___ *Whole-wheat durum*

TYPES OF SALT

- ☐ IODIZED TABLE SALT
- ☐ KOSHER MEDIUM-COARSE SALT
- ☐ PINK HIMALAYAN SALT
- ☐ VOLCANIC BLACK SALT
- ☐ MALDON SALT
- ☐ EXTRA FINE SEA SALT
- ☐ FRENCH GRAY SEA SALT
- ☐ SMOKED SEA SALT
- ☐ SEL GRIS

BAKING CONDITIONS

HUMIDITY

TEMPERATURE

STARTER DESCRIPTION

FINISHED LOAF DESCRIPTION

CRUMB DESCRIPTORS

- ☐ EVEN, "TIGHT" HOLES
- ☐ EVEN, MEDIUM HOLES
- ☐ IRREGULAR, LARGE HOLES
- ☐ DELICATE STRUCTURE
- ☐ AVERAGE STRUCTURE
- ☐ STURDY STRUCTURE
- ☐ TRANSLUCENT
- ☐ DENSE
- ☐ COOL AND CREAMY
- ☐ DRY OR DUSTY
- ☐ OTHER _____

CRUST DESCRIPTORS

- ☐ TENDER, GOLDEN
- ☐ SOFT, COMPRESSIBLE
- ☐ HARD, CRUSTY
- ☐ CARAMELIZED
- ☐ NUTTY
- ☐ BUTTERY
- ☐ OILY
- ☐ TOOTHSOME
- ☐ CRISPY
- ☐ OTHER _____

DATE _____

INGREDIENTS

TYPES OF FLOUR

- ☐ ALL-PURPOSE
- ☐ UNBLEACHED ALL-PURPOSE
- ☐ BREAD FLOUR
- ☐ UNBLEACHED WHEAT
  - ___ *Plus malted*
  - ___ *Low ash*
  - ___ *Malted All-purpose*
  - ___ *High-gluten*
- ☐ WHOLE-WHEAT
  - ___ *Fine*
  - ___ *High-protein fine*
  - ___ *Medium*
  - ___ *High-protein medium*
  - ___ *Coarse*
  - ___ *High-protein coarse*
  - ___ *Special medium/coarse*

- ☐ HARD WHITE WHOLE-WHEAT
- ☐ BROMATED HIGH-PROTEIN
- ☐ UNBLEACHED ENRICHED
- ☐ BLEACHED WHEAT
- ☐ ARTISAN BREAD
- ☐ IRISH-STYLE WHOLEMEAL
- ☐ HIGH-GLUTEN
- ☐ HIGH-EXTRACTION
  - ___ *Type 70 malted*
  - ___ *Stone ground type 80*
  - ___ *Type 80*
  - ___ *Old country type 85*
  - ___ *Old country type 85 malted*
- ☐ OTHER _____

- ☐ SPECIALTY
  - ___ *Barley*
  - ___ *Coarse cornmeal*
  - ___ *Fine cornmeal*
  - ___ *Polenta*
  - ___ *Flaxseed meal*
  - ___ *Millet*
  - ___ *Brown rice*
  - ___ *White rice*
  - ___ *Cream of rye*
  - ___ *Pumpernickel rye*
  - ___ *White rye*
  - ___ *Whole dark rye*
  - ___ *Spelt*
  - ___ *Semolina*
  - ___ *Whole durum*
  - ___ *Whole-wheat durum*

TYPES OF SALT

- ☐ IODIZED TABLE SALT
- ☐ KOSHER MEDIUM-COARSE SALT
- ☐ PINK HIMALAYAN SALT
- ☐ VOLCANIC BLACK SALT
- ☐ MALDON SALT
- ☐ EXTRA FINE SEA SALT
- ☐ FRENCH GRAY SEA SALT
- ☐ SMOKED SEA SALT
- ☐ SEL GRIS

BAKING CONDITIONS

HUMIDITY

TEMPERATURE

STARTER DESCRIPTION

FINISHED LOAF DESCRIPTION

CRUMB DESCRIPTORS

- ☐ EVEN, "TIGHT" HOLES
- ☐ EVEN, MEDIUM HOLES
- ☐ IRREGULAR, LARGE HOLES
- ☐ DELICATE STRUCTURE
- ☐ AVERAGE STRUCTURE
- ☐ STURDY STRUCTURE
- ☐ TRANSLUCENT
- ☐ DENSE
- ☐ COOL AND CREAMY
- ☐ DRY OR DUSTY
- ☐ OTHER _____

CRUST DESCRIPTORS

- ☐ TENDER, GOLDEN
- ☐ SOFT, COMPRESSIBLE
- ☐ HARD, CRUSTY
- ☐ CARAMELIZED
- ☐ NUTTY
- ☐ BUTTERY
- ☐ OILY
- ☐ TOOTHSOME
- ☐ CRISPY
- ☐ OTHER _____

DATE _____

INGREDIENTS

TYPES OF FLOUR

- ☐ ALL-PURPOSE
- ☐ UNBLEACHED ALL-PURPOSE
- ☐ BREAD FLOUR
- ☐ UNBLEACHED WHEAT
  - ___ *Plus malted*
  - ___ *Low ash*
  - ___ *Malted All-purpose*
  - ___ *High-gluten*
- ☐ WHOLE-WHEAT
  - ___ *Fine*
  - ___ *High-protein fine*
  - ___ *Medium*
  - ___ *High-protein medium*
  - ___ *Coarse*
  - ___ *High-protein coarse*
  - ___ *Special medium/coarse*

- ☐ HARD WHITE WHOLE-WHEAT
- ☐ BROMATED HIGH-PROTEIN
- ☐ UNBLEACHED ENRICHED
- ☐ BLEACHED WHEAT
- ☐ ARTISAN BREAD
- ☐ IRISH-STYLE WHOLEMEAL
- ☐ HIGH-GLUTEN
- ☐ HIGH-EXTRACTION
  - ___ *Type 70 malted*
  - ___ *Stone ground type 80*
  - ___ *Type 80*
  - ___ *Old country type 85*
  - ___ *Old country type 85 malted*
- ☐ OTHER _____

- ☐ SPECIALTY
  - ___ *Barley*
  - ___ *Coarse cornmeal*
  - ___ *Fine cornmeal*
  - ___ *Polenta*
  - ___ *Flaxseed meal*
  - ___ *Millet*
  - ___ *Brown rice*
  - ___ *White rice*
  - ___ *Cream of rye*
  - ___ *Pumpernickel rye*
  - ___ *White rye*
  - ___ *Whole dark rye*
  - ___ *Spelt*
  - ___ *Semolina*
  - ___ *Whole durum*
  - ___ *Whole-wheat durum*

TYPES OF SALT

- ☐ IODIZED TABLE SALT
- ☐ KOSHER MEDIUM-COARSE SALT
- ☐ PINK HIMALAYAN SALT
- ☐ VOLCANIC BLACK SALT
- ☐ MALDON SALT
- ☐ EXTRA FINE SEA SALT
- ☐ FRENCH GRAY SEA SALT
- ☐ SMOKED SEA SALT
- ☐ SEL GRIS

BAKING CONDITIONS

HUMIDITY

TEMPERATURE

STARTER DESCRIPTION

FINISHED LOAF DESCRIPTION

CRUMB DESCRIPTORS

- ☐ EVEN, "TIGHT" HOLES
- ☐ EVEN, MEDIUM HOLES
- ☐ IRREGULAR, LARGE HOLES
- ☐ DELICATE STRUCTURE
- ☐ AVERAGE STRUCTURE
- ☐ STURDY STRUCTURE
- ☐ TRANSLUCENT
- ☐ DENSE
- ☐ COOL AND CREAMY
- ☐ DRY OR DUSTY
- ☐ OTHER _____

CRUST DESCRIPTORS

- ☐ TENDER, GOLDEN
- ☐ SOFT, COMPRESSIBLE
- ☐ HARD, CRUSTY
- ☐ CARAMELIZED
- ☐ NUTTY
- ☐ BUTTERY
- ☐ OILY
- ☐ TOOTHSOME
- ☐ CRISPY
- ☐ OTHER _____

DATE _____

INGREDIENTS

TYPES OF FLOUR

- ☐ ALL-PURPOSE
- ☐ UNBLEACHED ALL-PURPOSE
- ☐ BREAD FLOUR
- ☐ UNBLEACHED WHEAT
  - ___ *Plus malted*
  - ___ *Low ash*
  - ___ *Malted All-purpose*
  - ___ *High-gluten*
- ☐ WHOLE-WHEAT
  - ___ *Fine*
  - ___ *High-protein fine*
  - ___ *Medium*
  - ___ *High-protein medium*
  - ___ *Coarse*
  - ___ *High-protein coarse*
  - ___ *Special medium/coarse*

- ☐ HARD WHITE WHOLE-WHEAT
- ☐ BROMATED HIGH-PROTEIN
- ☐ UNBLEACHED ENRICHED
- ☐ BLEACHED WHEAT
- ☐ ARTISAN BREAD
- ☐ IRISH-STYLE WHOLEMEAL
- ☐ HIGH-GLUTEN
- ☐ HIGH-EXTRACTION
  - ___ *Type 70 malted*
  - ___ *Stone ground type 80*
  - ___ *Type 80*
  - ___ *Old country type 85*
  - ___ *Old country type 85 malted*
- ☐ OTHER _____

- ☐ SPECIALTY
  - ___ *Barley*
  - ___ *Coarse cornmeal*
  - ___ *Fine cornmeal*
  - ___ *Polenta*
  - ___ *Flaxseed meal*
  - ___ *Millet*
  - ___ *Brown rice*
  - ___ *White rice*
  - ___ *Cream of rye*
  - ___ *Pumpernickel rye*
  - ___ *White rye*
  - ___ *Whole dark rye*
  - ___ *Spelt*
  - ___ *Semolina*
  - ___ *Whole durum*
  - ___ *Whole-wheat durum*

TYPES OF SALT

- ☐ IODIZED TABLE SALT
- ☐ KOSHER MEDIUM-COARSE SALT
- ☐ PINK HIMALAYAN SALT
- ☐ VOLCANIC BLACK SALT
- ☐ MALDON SALT
- ☐ EXTRA FINE SEA SALT
- ☐ FRENCH GRAY SEA SALT
- ☐ SMOKED SEA SALT
- ☐ SEL GRIS

BAKING CONDITIONS

HUMIDITY

TEMPERATURE

STARTER DESCRIPTION

FINISHED LOAF DESCRIPTION

CRUMB DESCRIPTORS

- ☐ EVEN, "TIGHT" HOLES
- ☐ EVEN, MEDIUM HOLES
- ☐ IRREGULAR, LARGE HOLES
- ☐ DELICATE STRUCTURE
- ☐ AVERAGE STRUCTURE
- ☐ STURDY STRUCTURE
- ☐ TRANSLUCENT
- ☐ DENSE
- ☐ COOL AND CREAMY
- ☐ DRY OR DUSTY
- ☐ OTHER _____

CRUST DESCRIPTORS

- ☐ TENDER, GOLDEN
- ☐ SOFT, COMPRESSIBLE
- ☐ HARD, CRUSTY
- ☐ CARAMELIZED
- ☐ NUTTY
- ☐ BUTTERY
- ☐ OILY
- ☐ TOOTHSOME
- ☐ CRISPY
- ☐ OTHER _____

DATE _____

INGREDIENTS

TYPES OF FLOUR

- ☐ ALL-PURPOSE
- ☐ UNBLEACHED ALL-PURPOSE
- ☐ BREAD FLOUR
- ☐ UNBLEACHED WHEAT
  - ___ *Plus malted*
  - ___ *Low ash*
  - ___ *Malted All-purpose*
  - ___ *High-gluten*
- ☐ WHOLE-WHEAT
  - ___ *Fine*
  - ___ *High-protein fine*
  - ___ *Medium*
  - ___ *High-protein medium*
  - ___ *Coarse*
  - ___ *High-protein coarse*
  - ___ *Special medium/coarse*

- ☐ HARD WHITE WHOLE-WHEAT
- ☐ BROMATED HIGH-PROTEIN
- ☐ UNBLEACHED ENRICHED
- ☐ BLEACHED WHEAT
- ☐ ARTISAN BREAD
- ☐ IRISH-STYLE WHOLEMEAL
- ☐ HIGH-GLUTEN
- ☐ HIGH-EXTRACTION
  - ___ *Type 70 malted*
  - ___ *Stone ground type 80*
  - ___ *Type 80*
  - ___ *Old country type 85*
  - ___ *Old country type 85 malted*
- ☐ OTHER _____

- ☐ SPECIALTY
  - ___ *Barley*
  - ___ *Coarse cornmeal*
  - ___ *Fine cornmeal*
  - ___ *Polenta*
  - ___ *Flaxseed meal*
  - ___ *Millet*
  - ___ *Brown rice*
  - ___ *White rice*
  - ___ *Cream of rye*
  - ___ *Pumpernickel rye*
  - ___ *White rye*
  - ___ *Whole dark rye*
  - ___ *Spelt*
  - ___ *Semolina*
  - ___ *Whole durum*
  - ___ *Whole-wheat durum*

TYPES OF SALT

- ☐ IODIZED TABLE SALT
- ☐ KOSHER MEDIUM-COARSE SALT
- ☐ PINK HIMALAYAN SALT
- ☐ VOLCANIC BLACK SALT
- ☐ MALDON SALT
- ☐ EXTRA FINE SEA SALT
- ☐ FRENCH GRAY SEA SALT
- ☐ SMOKED SEA SALT
- ☐ SEL GRIS

BAKING CONDITIONS

HUMIDITY

TEMPERATURE

STARTER DESCRIPTION

FINISHED LOAF DESCRIPTION

CRUMB DESCRIPTORS

- ☐ EVEN, "TIGHT" HOLES
- ☐ EVEN, MEDIUM HOLES
- ☐ IRREGULAR, LARGE HOLES
- ☐ DELICATE STRUCTURE
- ☐ AVERAGE STRUCTURE
- ☐ STURDY STRUCTURE
- ☐ TRANSLUCENT
- ☐ DENSE
- ☐ COOL AND CREAMY
- ☐ DRY OR DUSTY
- ☐ OTHER _____

CRUST DESCRIPTORS

- ☐ TENDER, GOLDEN
- ☐ SOFT, COMPRESSIBLE
- ☐ HARD, CRUSTY
- ☐ CARAMELIZED
- ☐ NUTTY
- ☐ BUTTERY
- ☐ OILY
- ☐ TOOTHSOME
- ☐ CRISPY
- ☐ OTHER _____

DATE _____

NOTES

INGREDIENTS

TYPES OF FLOUR

- ☐ ALL-PURPOSE
- ☐ UNBLEACHED ALL-PURPOSE
- ☐ BREAD FLOUR
- ☐ UNBLEACHED WHEAT
  - ___ *Plus malted*
  - ___ *Low ash*
  - ___ *Malted All-purpose*
  - ___ *High-gluten*
- ☐ WHOLE-WHEAT
  - ___ *Fine*
  - ___ *High-protein fine*
  - ___ *Medium*
  - ___ *High-protein medium*
  - ___ *Coarse*
  - ___ *High-protein coarse*
  - ___ *Special medium/coarse*

- ☐ HARD WHITE WHOLE-WHEAT
- ☐ BROMATED HIGH-PROTEIN
- ☐ UNBLEACHED ENRICHED
- ☐ BLEACHED WHEAT
- ☐ ARTISAN BREAD
- ☐ IRISH-STYLE WHOLEMEAL
- ☐ HIGH-GLUTEN
- ☐ HIGH-EXTRACTION
  - ___ *Type 70 malted*
  - ___ *Stone ground type 80*
  - ___ *Type 80*
  - ___ *Old country type 85*
  - ___ *Old country type 85 malted*
- ☐ OTHER _____

- ☐ SPECIALTY
  - ___ *Barley*
  - ___ *Coarse cornmeal*
  - ___ *Fine cornmeal*
  - ___ *Polenta*
  - ___ *Flaxseed meal*
  - ___ *Millet*
  - ___ *Brown rice*
  - ___ *White rice*
  - ___ *Cream of rye*
  - ___ *Pumpernickel rye*
  - ___ *White rye*
  - ___ *Whole dark rye*
  - ___ *Spelt*
  - ___ *Semolina*
  - ___ *Whole durum*
  - ___ *Whole-wheat durum*

TYPES OF SALT

- ☐ IODIZED TABLE SALT
- ☐ KOSHER MEDIUM-COARSE SALT
- ☐ PINK HIMALAYAN SALT
- ☐ VOLCANIC BLACK SALT
- ☐ MALDON SALT
- ☐ EXTRA FINE SEA SALT
- ☐ FRENCH GRAY SEA SALT
- ☐ SMOKED SEA SALT
- ☐ SEL GRIS

BAKING CONDITIONS

HUMIDITY

TEMPERATURE

STARTER DESCRIPTION

FINISHED LOAF DESCRIPTION

CRUMB DESCRIPTORS

- ☐ EVEN, "TIGHT" HOLES
- ☐ EVEN, MEDIUM HOLES
- ☐ IRREGULAR, LARGE HOLES
- ☐ DELICATE STRUCTURE
- ☐ AVERAGE STRUCTURE
- ☐ STURDY STRUCTURE
- ☐ TRANSLUCENT
- ☐ DENSE
- ☐ COOL AND CREAMY
- ☐ DRY OR DUSTY
- ☐ OTHER _____

CRUST DESCRIPTORS

- ☐ TENDER, GOLDEN
- ☐ SOFT, COMPRESSIBLE
- ☐ HARD, CRUSTY
- ☐ CARAMELIZED
- ☐ NUTTY
- ☐ BUTTERY
- ☐ OILY
- ☐ TOOTHSOME
- ☐ CRISPY
- ☐ OTHER _____

DATE _____

NOTES

INGREDIENTS

TYPES OF FLOUR

- [ ] ALL-PURPOSE
- [ ] UNBLEACHED ALL-PURPOSE
- [ ] BREAD FLOUR
- [ ] UNBLEACHED WHEAT
  - ___ *Plus malted*
  - ___ *Low ash*
  - ___ *Malted All-purpose*
  - ___ *High-gluten*
- [ ] WHOLE-WHEAT
  - ___ *Fine*
  - ___ *High-protein fine*
  - ___ *Medium*
  - ___ *High-protein medium*
  - ___ *Coarse*
  - ___ *High-protein coarse*
  - ___ *Special medium/coarse*

- [ ] HARD WHITE WHOLE-WHEAT
- [ ] BROMATED HIGH-PROTEIN
- [ ] UNBLEACHED ENRICHED
- [ ] BLEACHED WHEAT
- [ ] ARTISAN BREAD
- [ ] IRISH-STYLE WHOLEMEAL
- [ ] HIGH-GLUTEN
- [ ] HIGH-EXTRACTION
  - ___ *Type 70 malted*
  - ___ *Stone ground type 80*
  - ___ *Type 80*
  - ___ *Old country type 85*
  - ___ *Old country type 85 malted*
- [ ] OTHER _____

- [ ] SPECIALTY
  - ___ *Barley*
  - ___ *Coarse cornmeal*
  - ___ *Fine cornmeal*
  - ___ *Polenta*
  - ___ *Flaxseed meal*
  - ___ *Millet*
  - ___ *Brown rice*
  - ___ *White rice*
  - ___ *Cream of rye*
  - ___ *Pumpernickel rye*
  - ___ *White rye*
  - ___ *Whole dark rye*
  - ___ *Spelt*
  - ___ *Semolina*
  - ___ *Whole durum*
  - ___ *Whole-wheat durum*

TYPES OF SALT

- [ ] IODIZED TABLE SALT
- [ ] KOSHER MEDIUM-COARSE SALT
- [ ] PINK HIMALAYAN SALT
- [ ] VOLCANIC BLACK SALT
- [ ] MALDON SALT
- [ ] EXTRA FINE SEA SALT
- [ ] FRENCH GRAY SEA SALT
- [ ] SMOKED SEA SALT
- [ ] SEL GRIS

BAKING CONDITIONS

HUMIDITY

TEMPERATURE

STARTER DESCRIPTION

FINISHED LOAF DESCRIPTION

CRUMB DESCRIPTORS

- [ ] EVEN, "TIGHT" HOLES
- [ ] EVEN, MEDIUM HOLES
- [ ] IRREGULAR, LARGE HOLES
- [ ] DELICATE STRUCTURE
- [ ] AVERAGE STRUCTURE
- [ ] STURDY STRUCTURE
- [ ] TRANSLUCENT
- [ ] DENSE
- [ ] COOL AND CREAMY
- [ ] DRY OR DUSTY
- [ ] OTHER _____

CRUST DESCRIPTORS

- [ ] TENDER, GOLDEN
- [ ] SOFT, COMPRESSIBLE
- [ ] HARD, CRUSTY
- [ ] CARAMELIZED
- [ ] NUTTY
- [ ] BUTTERY
- [ ] OILY
- [ ] TOOTHSOME
- [ ] CRISPY
- [ ] OTHER _____

DATE _____

NOTES

INGREDIENTS

TYPES OF FLOUR

- ☐ ALL-PURPOSE
- ☐ UNBLEACHED ALL-PURPOSE
- ☐ BREAD FLOUR
- ☐ UNBLEACHED WHEAT
  - ___ *Plus malted*
  - ___ *Low ash*
  - ___ *Malted All-purpose*
  - ___ *High-gluten*
- ☐ WHOLE-WHEAT
  - ___ *Fine*
  - ___ *High-protein fine*
  - ___ *Medium*
  - ___ *High-protein medium*
  - ___ *Coarse*
  - ___ *High-protein coarse*
  - ___ *Special medium/coarse*

- ☐ HARD WHITE WHOLE-WHEAT
- ☐ BROMATED HIGH-PROTEIN
- ☐ UNBLEACHED ENRICHED
- ☐ BLEACHED WHEAT
- ☐ ARTISAN BREAD
- ☐ IRISH-STYLE WHOLEMEAL
- ☐ HIGH-GLUTEN
- ☐ HIGH-EXTRACTION
  - ___ *Type 70 malted*
  - ___ *Stone ground type 80*
  - ___ *Type 80*
  - ___ *Old country type 85*
  - ___ *Old country type 85 malted*
- ☐ OTHER _____

- ☐ SPECIALTY
  - ___ *Barley*
  - ___ *Coarse cornmeal*
  - ___ *Fine cornmeal*
  - ___ *Polenta*
  - ___ *Flaxseed meal*
  - ___ *Millet*
  - ___ *Brown rice*
  - ___ *White rice*
  - ___ *Cream of rye*
  - ___ *Pumpernickel rye*
  - ___ *White rye*
  - ___ *Whole dark rye*
  - ___ *Spelt*
  - ___ *Semolina*
  - ___ *Whole durum*
  - ___ *Whole-wheat durum*

TYPES OF SALT

- ☐ IODIZED TABLE SALT
- ☐ KOSHER MEDIUM-COARSE SALT
- ☐ PINK HIMALAYAN SALT
- ☐ VOLCANIC BLACK SALT
- ☐ MALDON SALT
- ☐ EXTRA FINE SEA SALT
- ☐ FRENCH GRAY SEA SALT
- ☐ SMOKED SEA SALT
- ☐ SEL GRIS

BAKING CONDITIONS

HUMIDITY

TEMPERATURE

STARTER DESCRIPTION

FINISHED LOAF DESCRIPTION

CRUMB DESCRIPTORS

- ☐ EVEN, "TIGHT" HOLES
- ☐ EVEN, MEDIUM HOLES
- ☐ IRREGULAR, LARGE HOLES
- ☐ DELICATE STRUCTURE
- ☐ AVERAGE STRUCTURE
- ☐ STURDY STRUCTURE
- ☐ TRANSLUCENT
- ☐ DENSE
- ☐ COOL AND CREAMY
- ☐ DRY OR DUSTY
- ☐ OTHER _____

CRUST DESCRIPTORS

- ☐ TENDER, GOLDEN
- ☐ SOFT, COMPRESSIBLE
- ☐ HARD, CRUSTY
- ☐ CARAMELIZED
- ☐ NUTTY
- ☐ BUTTERY
- ☐ OILY
- ☐ TOOTHSOME
- ☐ CRISPY
- ☐ OTHER _____

DATE _____

INGREDIENTS

TYPES OF FLOUR

- ☐ ALL-PURPOSE
- ☐ UNBLEACHED ALL-PURPOSE
- ☐ BREAD FLOUR
- ☐ UNBLEACHED WHEAT
  - ___ *Plus malted*
  - ___ *Low ash*
  - ___ *Malted All-purpose*
  - ___ *High-gluten*
- ☐ WHOLE-WHEAT
  - ___ *Fine*
  - ___ *High-protein fine*
  - ___ *Medium*
  - ___ *High-protein medium*
  - ___ *Coarse*
  - ___ *High-protein coarse*
  - ___ *Special medium/coarse*

- ☐ HARD WHITE WHOLE-WHEAT
- ☐ BROMATED HIGH-PROTEIN
- ☐ UNBLEACHED ENRICHED
- ☐ BLEACHED WHEAT
- ☐ ARTISAN BREAD
- ☐ IRISH-STYLE WHOLEMEAL
- ☐ HIGH-GLUTEN
- ☐ HIGH-EXTRACTION
  - ___ *Type 70 malted*
  - ___ *Stone ground type 80*
  - ___ *Type 80*
  - ___ *Old country type 85*
  - ___ *Old country type 85 malted*
- ☐ OTHER _____

- ☐ SPECIALTY
  - ___ *Barley*
  - ___ *Coarse cornmeal*
  - ___ *Fine cornmeal*
  - ___ *Polenta*
  - ___ *Flaxseed meal*
  - ___ *Millet*
  - ___ *Brown rice*
  - ___ *White rice*
  - ___ *Cream of rye*
  - ___ *Pumpernickel rye*
  - ___ *White rye*
  - ___ *Whole dark rye*
  - ___ *Spelt*
  - ___ *Semolina*
  - ___ *Whole durum*
  - ___ *Whole-wheat durum*

TYPES OF SALT

- ☐ IODIZED TABLE SALT
- ☐ KOSHER MEDIUM-COARSE SALT
- ☐ PINK HIMALAYAN SALT
- ☐ VOLCANIC BLACK SALT
- ☐ MALDON SALT
- ☐ EXTRA FINE SEA SALT
- ☐ FRENCH GRAY SEA SALT
- ☐ SMOKED SEA SALT
- ☐ SEL GRIS

BAKING CONDITIONS

HUMIDITY

TEMPERATURE

STARTER DESCRIPTION

FINISHED LOAF DESCRIPTION

CRUMB DESCRIPTORS

- ☐ EVEN, "TIGHT" HOLES
- ☐ EVEN, MEDIUM HOLES
- ☐ IRREGULAR, LARGE HOLES
- ☐ DELICATE STRUCTURE
- ☐ AVERAGE STRUCTURE
- ☐ STURDY STRUCTURE
- ☐ TRANSLUCENT
- ☐ DENSE
- ☐ COOL AND CREAMY
- ☐ DRY OR DUSTY
- ☐ OTHER _____

CRUST DESCRIPTORS

- ☐ TENDER, GOLDEN
- ☐ SOFT, COMPRESSIBLE
- ☐ HARD, CRUSTY
- ☐ CARAMELIZED
- ☐ NUTTY
- ☐ BUTTERY
- ☐ OILY
- ☐ TOOTHSOME
- ☐ CRISPY
- ☐ OTHER _____

DATE _____

NOTES

INGREDIENTS

TYPES OF FLOUR

- ☐ ALL-PURPOSE
- ☐ UNBLEACHED ALL-PURPOSE
- ☐ BREAD FLOUR
- ☐ UNBLEACHED WHEAT
  - ___ *Plus malted*
  - ___ *Low ash*
  - ___ *Malted All-purpose*
  - ___ *High-gluten*
- ☐ WHOLE-WHEAT
  - ___ *Fine*
  - ___ *High-protein fine*
  - ___ *Medium*
  - ___ *High-protein medium*
  - ___ *Coarse*
  - ___ *High-protein coarse*
  - ___ *Special medium/coarse*

- ☐ HARD WHITE WHOLE-WHEAT
- ☐ BROMATED HIGH-PROTEIN
- ☐ UNBLEACHED ENRICHED
- ☐ BLEACHED WHEAT
- ☐ ARTISAN BREAD
- ☐ IRISH-STYLE WHOLEMEAL
- ☐ HIGH-GLUTEN
- ☐ HIGH-EXTRACTION
  - ___ *Type 70 malted*
  - ___ *Stone ground type 80*
  - ___ *Type 80*
  - ___ *Old country type 85*
  - ___ *Old country type 85 malted*
- ☐ OTHER _____

- ☐ SPECIALTY
  - ___ *Barley*
  - ___ *Coarse cornmeal*
  - ___ *Fine cornmeal*
  - ___ *Polenta*
  - ___ *Flaxseed meal*
  - ___ *Millet*
  - ___ *Brown rice*
  - ___ *White rice*
  - ___ *Cream of rye*
  - ___ *Pumpernickel rye*
  - ___ *White rye*
  - ___ *Whole dark rye*
  - ___ *Spelt*
  - ___ *Semolina*
  - ___ *Whole durum*
  - ___ *Whole-wheat durum*

TYPES OF SALT

- ☐ IODIZED TABLE SALT
- ☐ KOSHER MEDIUM-COARSE SALT
- ☐ PINK HIMALAYAN SALT
- ☐ VOLCANIC BLACK SALT
- ☐ MALDON SALT
- ☐ EXTRA FINE SEA SALT
- ☐ FRENCH GRAY SEA SALT
- ☐ SMOKED SEA SALT
- ☐ SEL GRIS

BAKING CONDITIONS

HUMIDITY

TEMPERATURE

STARTER DESCRIPTION

FINISHED LOAF DESCRIPTION

CRUMB DESCRIPTORS

- ☐ EVEN, "TIGHT" HOLES
- ☐ EVEN, MEDIUM HOLES
- ☐ IRREGULAR, LARGE HOLES
- ☐ DELICATE STRUCTURE
- ☐ AVERAGE STRUCTURE
- ☐ STURDY STRUCTURE
- ☐ TRANSLUCENT
- ☐ DENSE
- ☐ COOL AND CREAMY
- ☐ DRY OR DUSTY
- ☐ OTHER _____

CRUST DESCRIPTORS

- ☐ TENDER, GOLDEN
- ☐ SOFT, COMPRESSIBLE
- ☐ HARD, CRUSTY
- ☐ CARAMELIZED
- ☐ NUTTY
- ☐ BUTTERY
- ☐ OILY
- ☐ TOOTHSOME
- ☐ CRISPY
- ☐ OTHER _____

DATE _____

INGREDIENTS

TYPES OF FLOUR

- ☐ ALL-PURPOSE
- ☐ UNBLEACHED ALL-PURPOSE
- ☐ BREAD FLOUR
- ☐ UNBLEACHED WHEAT
  - ___ *Plus malted*
  - ___ *Low ash*
  - ___ *Malted All-purpose*
  - ___ *High-gluten*
- ☐ WHOLE-WHEAT
  - ___ *Fine*
  - ___ *High-protein fine*
  - ___ *Medium*
  - ___ *High-protein medium*
  - ___ *Coarse*
  - ___ *High-protein coarse*
  - ___ *Special medium/coarse*

- ☐ HARD WHITE WHOLE-WHEAT
- ☐ BROMATED HIGH-PROTEIN
- ☐ UNBLEACHED ENRICHED
- ☐ BLEACHED WHEAT
- ☐ ARTISAN BREAD
- ☐ IRISH-STYLE WHOLEMEAL
- ☐ HIGH-GLUTEN
- ☐ HIGH-EXTRACTION
  - ___ *Type 70 malted*
  - ___ *Stone ground type 80*
  - ___ *Type 80*
  - ___ *Old country type 85*
  - ___ *Old country type 85 malted*
- ☐ OTHER _____

- ☐ SPECIALTY
  - ___ *Barley*
  - ___ *Coarse cornmeal*
  - ___ *Fine cornmeal*
  - ___ *Polenta*
  - ___ *Flaxseed meal*
  - ___ *Millet*
  - ___ *Brown rice*
  - ___ *White rice*
  - ___ *Cream of rye*
  - ___ *Pumpernickel rye*
  - ___ *White rye*
  - ___ *Whole dark rye*
  - ___ *Spelt*
  - ___ *Semolina*
  - ___ *Whole durum*
  - ___ *Whole-wheat durum*

TYPES OF SALT

- ☐ IODIZED TABLE SALT
- ☐ KOSHER MEDIUM-COARSE SALT
- ☐ PINK HIMALAYAN SALT
- ☐ VOLCANIC BLACK SALT
- ☐ MALDON SALT
- ☐ EXTRA FINE SEA SALT
- ☐ FRENCH GRAY SEA SALT
- ☐ SMOKED SEA SALT
- ☐ SEL GRIS

BAKING CONDITIONS

HUMIDITY

TEMPERATURE

STARTER DESCRIPTION

FINISHED LOAF DESCRIPTION

CRUMB DESCRIPTORS

- ☐ EVEN, "TIGHT" HOLES
- ☐ EVEN, MEDIUM HOLES
- ☐ IRREGULAR, LARGE HOLES
- ☐ DELICATE STRUCTURE
- ☐ AVERAGE STRUCTURE
- ☐ STURDY STRUCTURE
- ☐ TRANSLUCENT
- ☐ DENSE
- ☐ COOL AND CREAMY
- ☐ DRY OR DUSTY
- ☐ OTHER _____

CRUST DESCRIPTORS

- ☐ TENDER, GOLDEN
- ☐ SOFT, COMPRESSIBLE
- ☐ HARD, CRUSTY
- ☐ CARAMELIZED
- ☐ NUTTY
- ☐ BUTTERY
- ☐ OILY
- ☐ TOOTHSOME
- ☐ CRISPY
- ☐ OTHER _____

DATE _____

INGREDIENTS

TYPES OF FLOUR

- ☐ ALL-PURPOSE
- ☐ UNBLEACHED ALL-PURPOSE
- ☐ BREAD FLOUR
- ☐ UNBLEACHED WHEAT
  - ___ *Plus malted*
  - ___ *Low ash*
  - ___ *Malted All-purpose*
  - ___ *High-gluten*
- ☐ WHOLE-WHEAT
  - ___ *Fine*
  - ___ *High-protein fine*
  - ___ *Medium*
  - ___ *High-protein medium*
  - ___ *Coarse*
  - ___ *High-protein coarse*
  - ___ *Special medium/coarse*

- ☐ HARD WHITE WHOLE-WHEAT
- ☐ BROMATED HIGH-PROTEIN
- ☐ UNBLEACHED ENRICHED
- ☐ BLEACHED WHEAT
- ☐ ARTISAN BREAD
- ☐ IRISH-STYLE WHOLEMEAL
- ☐ HIGH-GLUTEN
- ☐ HIGH-EXTRACTION
  - ___ *Type 70 malted*
  - ___ *Stone ground type 80*
  - ___ *Type 80*
  - ___ *Old country type 85*
  - ___ *Old country type 85 malted*
- ☐ OTHER _____

- ☐ SPECIALTY
  - ___ *Barley*
  - ___ *Coarse cornmeal*
  - ___ *Fine cornmeal*
  - ___ *Polenta*
  - ___ *Flaxseed meal*
  - ___ *Millet*
  - ___ *Brown rice*
  - ___ *White rice*
  - ___ *Cream of rye*
  - ___ *Pumpernickel rye*
  - ___ *White rye*
  - ___ *Whole dark rye*
  - ___ *Spelt*
  - ___ *Semolina*
  - ___ *Whole durum*
  - ___ *Whole-wheat durum*

TYPES OF SALT

- ☐ IODIZED TABLE SALT
- ☐ KOSHER MEDIUM-COARSE SALT
- ☐ PINK HIMALAYAN SALT
- ☐ VOLCANIC BLACK SALT
- ☐ MALDON SALT
- ☐ EXTRA FINE SEA SALT
- ☐ FRENCH GRAY SEA SALT
- ☐ SMOKED SEA SALT
- ☐ SEL GRIS

BAKING CONDITIONS

HUMIDITY

TEMPERATURE

STARTER DESCRIPTION

FINISHED LOAF DESCRIPTION

CRUMB DESCRIPTORS

- ☐ EVEN, "TIGHT" HOLES
- ☐ EVEN, MEDIUM HOLES
- ☐ IRREGULAR, LARGE HOLES
- ☐ DELICATE STRUCTURE
- ☐ AVERAGE STRUCTURE
- ☐ STURDY STRUCTURE
- ☐ TRANSLUCENT
- ☐ DENSE
- ☐ COOL AND CREAMY
- ☐ DRY OR DUSTY
- ☐ OTHER _____

CRUST DESCRIPTORS

- ☐ TENDER, GOLDEN
- ☐ SOFT, COMPRESSIBLE
- ☐ HARD, CRUSTY
- ☐ CARAMELIZED
- ☐ NUTTY
- ☐ BUTTERY
- ☐ OILY
- ☐ TOOTHSOME
- ☐ CRISPY
- ☐ OTHER _____

DATE _____

INGREDIENTS

TYPES OF FLOUR

- ☐ ALL-PURPOSE
- ☐ UNBLEACHED ALL-PURPOSE
- ☐ BREAD FLOUR
- ☐ UNBLEACHED WHEAT
  - ___ *Plus malted*
  - ___ *Low ash*
  - ___ *Malted All-purpose*
  - ___ *High-gluten*
- ☐ WHOLE-WHEAT
  - ___ *Fine*
  - ___ *High-protein fine*
  - ___ *Medium*
  - ___ *High-protein medium*
  - ___ *Coarse*
  - ___ *High-protein coarse*
  - ___ *Special medium/coarse*

- ☐ HARD WHITE WHOLE-WHEAT
- ☐ BROMATED HIGH-PROTEIN
- ☐ UNBLEACHED ENRICHED
- ☐ BLEACHED WHEAT
- ☐ ARTISAN BREAD
- ☐ IRISH-STYLE WHOLEMEAL
- ☐ HIGH-GLUTEN
- ☐ HIGH-EXTRACTION
  - ___ *Type 70 malted*
  - ___ *Stone ground type 80*
  - ___ *Type 80*
  - ___ *Old country type 85*
  - ___ *Old country type 85 malted*
- ☐ OTHER _____

- ☐ SPECIALTY
  - ___ *Barley*
  - ___ *Coarse cornmeal*
  - ___ *Fine cornmeal*
  - ___ *Polenta*
  - ___ *Flaxseed meal*
  - ___ *Millet*
  - ___ *Brown rice*
  - ___ *White rice*
  - ___ *Cream of rye*
  - ___ *Pumpernickel rye*
  - ___ *White rye*
  - ___ *Whole dark rye*
  - ___ *Spelt*
  - ___ *Semolina*
  - ___ *Whole durum*
  - ___ *Whole-wheat durum*

TYPES OF SALT

- ☐ IODIZED TABLE SALT
- ☐ KOSHER MEDIUM-COARSE SALT
- ☐ PINK HIMALAYAN SALT
- ☐ VOLCANIC BLACK SALT
- ☐ MALDON SALT
- ☐ EXTRA FINE SEA SALT
- ☐ FRENCH GRAY SEA SALT
- ☐ SMOKED SEA SALT
- ☐ SEL GRIS

BAKING CONDITIONS

HUMIDITY

TEMPERATURE

STARTER DESCRIPTION

FINISHED LOAF DESCRIPTION

CRUMB DESCRIPTORS

- ☐ EVEN, "TIGHT" HOLES
- ☐ EVEN, MEDIUM HOLES
- ☐ IRREGULAR, LARGE HOLES
- ☐ DELICATE STRUCTURE
- ☐ AVERAGE STRUCTURE
- ☐ STURDY STRUCTURE
- ☐ TRANSLUCENT
- ☐ DENSE
- ☐ COOL AND CREAMY
- ☐ DRY OR DUSTY
- ☐ OTHER _____

CRUST DESCRIPTORS

- ☐ TENDER, GOLDEN
- ☐ SOFT, COMPRESSIBLE
- ☐ HARD, CRUSTY
- ☐ CARAMELIZED
- ☐ NUTTY
- ☐ BUTTERY
- ☐ OILY
- ☐ TOOTHSOME
- ☐ CRISPY
- ☐ OTHER _____

DATE _____

NOTES

INGREDIENTS

TYPES OF FLOUR

- ☐ ALL-PURPOSE
- ☐ UNBLEACHED ALL-PURPOSE
- ☐ BREAD FLOUR
- ☐ UNBLEACHED WHEAT
  - ___ *Plus malted*
  - ___ *Low ash*
  - ___ *Malted All-purpose*
  - ___ *High-gluten*
- ☐ WHOLE-WHEAT
  - ___ *Fine*
  - ___ *High-protein fine*
  - ___ *Medium*
  - ___ *High-protein medium*
  - ___ *Coarse*
  - ___ *High-protein coarse*
  - ___ *Special medium/coarse*

- ☐ HARD WHITE WHOLE-WHEAT
- ☐ BROMATED HIGH-PROTEIN
- ☐ UNBLEACHED ENRICHED
- ☐ BLEACHED WHEAT
- ☐ ARTISAN BREAD
- ☐ IRISH-STYLE WHOLEMEAL
- ☐ HIGH-GLUTEN
- ☐ HIGH-EXTRACTION
  - ___ *Type 70 malted*
  - ___ *Stone ground type 80*
  - ___ *Type 80*
  - ___ *Old country type 85*
  - ___ *Old country type 85 malted*
- ☐ OTHER _____

- ☐ SPECIALTY
  - ___ *Barley*
  - ___ *Coarse cornmeal*
  - ___ *Fine cornmeal*
  - ___ *Polenta*
  - ___ *Flaxseed meal*
  - ___ *Millet*
  - ___ *Brown rice*
  - ___ *White rice*
  - ___ *Cream of rye*
  - ___ *Pumpernickel rye*
  - ___ *White rye*
  - ___ *Whole dark rye*
  - ___ *Spelt*
  - ___ *Semolina*
  - ___ *Whole durum*
  - ___ *Whole-wheat durum*

TYPES OF SALT

- ☐ IODIZED TABLE SALT
- ☐ KOSHER MEDIUM-COARSE SALT
- ☐ PINK HIMALAYAN SALT
- ☐ VOLCANIC BLACK SALT
- ☐ MALDON SALT
- ☐ EXTRA FINE SEA SALT
- ☐ FRENCH GRAY SEA SALT
- ☐ SMOKED SEA SALT
- ☐ SEL GRIS

BAKING CONDITIONS

HUMIDITY

TEMPERATURE

STARTER DESCRIPTION

FINISHED LOAF DESCRIPTION

CRUMB DESCRIPTORS

- ☐ EVEN, "TIGHT" HOLES
- ☐ EVEN, MEDIUM HOLES
- ☐ IRREGULAR, LARGE HOLES
- ☐ DELICATE STRUCTURE
- ☐ AVERAGE STRUCTURE
- ☐ STURDY STRUCTURE
- ☐ TRANSLUCENT
- ☐ DENSE
- ☐ COOL AND CREAMY
- ☐ DRY OR DUSTY
- ☐ OTHER _____

CRUST DESCRIPTORS

- ☐ TENDER, GOLDEN
- ☐ SOFT, COMPRESSIBLE
- ☐ HARD, CRUSTY
- ☐ CARAMELIZED
- ☐ NUTTY
- ☐ BUTTERY
- ☐ OILY
- ☐ TOOTHSOME
- ☐ CRISPY
- ☐ OTHER _____

DATE _____

NOTES

INGREDIENTS

TYPES OF FLOUR

- ☐ ALL-PURPOSE
- ☐ UNBLEACHED ALL-PURPOSE
- ☐ BREAD FLOUR
- ☐ UNBLEACHED WHEAT
  - ___ *Plus malted*
  - ___ *Low ash*
  - ___ *Malted All-purpose*
  - ___ *High-gluten*
- ☐ WHOLE-WHEAT
  - ___ *Fine*
  - ___ *High-protein fine*
  - ___ *Medium*
  - ___ *High-protein medium*
  - ___ *Coarse*
  - ___ *High-protein coarse*
  - ___ *Special medium/coarse*

- ☐ HARD WHITE WHOLE-WHEAT
- ☐ BROMATED HIGH-PROTEIN
- ☐ UNBLEACHED ENRICHED
- ☐ BLEACHED WHEAT
- ☐ ARTISAN BREAD
- ☐ IRISH-STYLE WHOLEMEAL
- ☐ HIGH-GLUTEN
- ☐ HIGH-EXTRACTION
  - ___ *Type 70 malted*
  - ___ *Stone ground type 80*
  - ___ *Type 80*
  - ___ *Old country type 85*
  - ___ *Old country type 85 malted*
- ☐ OTHER _____

- ☐ SPECIALTY
  - ___ *Barley*
  - ___ *Coarse cornmeal*
  - ___ *Fine cornmeal*
  - ___ *Polenta*
  - ___ *Flaxseed meal*
  - ___ *Millet*
  - ___ *Brown rice*
  - ___ *White rice*
  - ___ *Cream of rye*
  - ___ *Pumpernickel rye*
  - ___ *White rye*
  - ___ *Whole durk rye*
  - ___ *Spelt*
  - ___ *Semolina*
  - ___ *Whole durum*
  - ___ *Whole-wheat durum*

TYPES OF SALT

- ☐ IODIZED TABLE SALT
- ☐ KOSHER MEDIUM-COARSE SALT
- ☐ PINK HIMALAYAN SALT
- ☐ VOLCANIC BLACK SALT
- ☐ MALDON SALT
- ☐ EXTRA FINE SEA SALT
- ☐ FRENCH GRAY SEA SALT
- ☐ SMOKED SEA SALT
- ☐ SEL GRIS

BAKING CONDITIONS

HUMIDITY

TEMPERATURE

STARTER DESCRIPTION

FINISHED LOAF DESCRIPTION

CRUMB DESCRIPTORS

- ☐ EVEN, "TIGHT" HOLES
- ☐ EVEN, MEDIUM HOLES
- ☐ IRREGULAR, LARGE HOLES
- ☐ DELICATE STRUCTURE
- ☐ AVERAGE STRUCTURE
- ☐ STURDY STRUCTURE
- ☐ TRANSLUCENT
- ☐ DENSE
- ☐ COOL AND CREAMY
- ☐ DRY OR DUSTY
- ☐ OTHER _____

CRUST DESCRIPTORS

- ☐ TENDER, GOLDEN
- ☐ SOFT, COMPRESSIBLE
- ☐ HARD, CRUSTY
- ☐ CARAMELIZED
- ☐ NUTTY
- ☐ BUTTERY
- ☐ OILY
- ☐ TOOTHSOME
- ☐ CRISPY
- ☐ OTHER _____

DATE _____

NOTES

INGREDIENTS

TYPES OF FLOUR

- ☐ ALL-PURPOSE
- ☐ UNBLEACHED ALL-PURPOSE
- ☐ BREAD FLOUR
- ☐ UNBLEACHED WHEAT
  - ___ *Plus malted*
  - ___ *Low ash*
  - ___ *Malted All-purpose*
  - ___ *High-gluten*
- ☐ WHOLE-WHEAT
  - ___ *Fine*
  - ___ *High-protein fine*
  - ___ *Medium*
  - ___ *High-protein medium*
  - ___ *Coarse*
  - ___ *High-protein coarse*
  - ___ *Special medium/coarse*

- ☐ HARD WHITE WHOLE-WHEAT
- ☐ BROMATED HIGH-PROTEIN
- ☐ UNBLEACHED ENRICHED
- ☐ BLEACHED WHEAT
- ☐ ARTISAN BREAD
- ☐ IRISH-STYLE WHOLEMEAL
- ☐ HIGH-GLUTEN
- ☐ HIGH-EXTRACTION
  - ___ *Type 70 malted*
  - ___ *Stone ground type 80*
  - ___ *Type 80*
  - ___ *Old country type 85*
  - ___ *Old country type 85 malted*
- ☐ OTHER _____

- ☐ SPECIALTY
  - ___ *Barley*
  - ___ *Coarse cornmeal*
  - ___ *Fine cornmeal*
  - ___ *Polenta*
  - ___ *Flaxseed meal*
  - ___ *Millet*
  - ___ *Brown rice*
  - ___ *White rice*
  - ___ *Cream of rye*
  - ___ *Pumpernickel rye*
  - ___ *White rye*
  - ___ *Whole dark rye*
  - ___ *Spelt*
  - ___ *Semolina*
  - ___ *Whole durum*
  - ___ *Whole-wheat durum*

TYPES OF SALT

- ☐ IODIZED TABLE SALT
- ☐ KOSHER MEDIUM-COARSE SALT
- ☐ PINK HIMALAYAN SALT
- ☐ VOLCANIC BLACK SALT
- ☐ MALDON SALT
- ☐ EXTRA FINE SEA SALT
- ☐ FRENCH GRAY SEA SALT
- ☐ SMOKED SEA SALT
- ☐ SEL GRIS

BAKING CONDITIONS

HUMIDITY

TEMPERATURE

STARTER DESCRIPTION

FINISHED LOAF DESCRIPTION

CRUMB DESCRIPTORS

- ☐ EVEN, "TIGHT" HOLES
- ☐ EVEN, MEDIUM HOLES
- ☐ IRREGULAR, LARGE HOLES
- ☐ DELICATE STRUCTURE
- ☐ AVERAGE STRUCTURE
- ☐ STURDY STRUCTURE
- ☐ TRANSLUCENT
- ☐ DENSE
- ☐ COOL AND CREAMY
- ☐ DRY OR DUSTY
- ☐ OTHER _____

CRUST DESCRIPTORS

- ☐ TENDER, GOLDEN
- ☐ SOFT, COMPRESSIBLE
- ☐ HARD, CRUSTY
- ☐ CARAMELIZED
- ☐ NUTTY
- ☐ BUTTERY
- ☐ OILY
- ☐ TOOTHSOME
- ☐ CRISPY
- ☐ OTHER _____

DATE _____

NOTES

INGREDIENTS

TYPES OF FLOUR

- ☐ ALL-PURPOSE
- ☐ UNBLEACHED ALL-PURPOSE
- ☐ BREAD FLOUR
- ☐ UNBLEACHED WHEAT
    - ___ *Plus malted*
    - ___ *Low ash*
    - ___ *Malted All-purpose*
    - ___ *High-gluten*
- ☐ WHOLE-WHEAT
    - ___ *Fine*
    - ___ *High protein fine*
    - ___ *Medium*
    - ___ *High-protein medium*
    - ___ *Coarse*
    - ___ *High-protein coarse*
    - ___ *Special medium/coarse*

- ☐ HARD WHITE WHOLE-WHEAT
- ☐ BROMATED HIGH-PROTEIN
- ☐ UNBLEACHED ENRICHED
- ☐ BLEACHED WHEAT
- ☐ ARTISAN BREAD
- ☐ IRISH-STYLE WHOLEMEAL
- ☐ HIGH-GLUTEN
- ☐ HIGH-EXTRACTION
    - ___ *Type 70 malted*
    - ___ *Stone ground type 80*
    - ___ *Type 80*
    - ___ *Old country type 85*
    - ___ *Old country type 85 malted*
- ☐ OTHER _____

- ☐ SPECIALTY
    - ___ *Barley*
    - ___ *Coarse cornmeal*
    - ___ *Fine cornmeal*
    - ___ *Polenta*
    - ___ *Flaxseed meal*
    - ___ *Millet*
    - ___ *Brown rice*
    - ___ *White rice*
    - ___ *Cream of rye*
    - ___ *Pumpernickel rye*
    - ___ *White rye*
    - ___ *Whole dark rye*
    - ___ *Spelt*
    - ___ *Semolina*
    - ___ *Whole durum*
    - ___ *Whole-wheat durum*

TYPES OF SALT

- ☐ IODIZED TABLE SALT
- ☐ KOSHER MEDIUM-COARSE SALT
- ☐ PINK HIMALAYAN SALT
- ☐ VOLCANIC BLACK SALT
- ☐ MALDON SALT
- ☐ EXTRA FINE SEA SALT
- ☐ FRENCH GRAY SEA SALT
- ☐ SMOKED SEA SALT
- ☐ SEL GRIS

BAKING CONDITIONS

HUMIDITY

TEMPERATURE

STARTER DESCRIPTION

FINISHED LOAF DESCRIPTION

CRUMB DESCRIPTORS

- ☐ EVEN, "TIGHT" HOLES
- ☐ EVEN, MEDIUM HOLES
- ☐ IRREGULAR, LARGE HOLES
- ☐ DELICATE STRUCTURE
- ☐ AVERAGE STRUCTURE
- ☐ STURDY STRUCTURE
- ☐ TRANSLUCENT
- ☐ DENSE
- ☐ COOL AND CREAMY
- ☐ DRY OR DUSTY
- ☐ OTHER _____

CRUST DESCRIPTORS

- ☐ TENDER, GOLDEN
- ☐ SOFT, COMPRESSIBLE
- ☐ HARD, CRUSTY
- ☐ CARAMELIZED
- ☐ NUTTY
- ☐ BUTTERY
- ☐ OILY
- ☐ TOOTHSOME
- ☐ CRISPY
- ☐ OTHER _____

DATE _____

INGREDIENTS

TYPES OF FLOUR

- ☐ ALL-PURPOSE
- ☐ UNBLEACHED ALL-PURPOSE
- ☐ BREAD FLOUR
- ☐ UNBLEACHED WHEAT
  - ___ *Plus malted*
  - ___ *Low ash*
  - ___ *Malted All-purpose*
  - ___ *High-gluten*
- ☐ WHOLE-WHEAT
  - ___ *Fine*
  - ___ *High-protein fine*
  - ___ *Medium*
  - ___ *High-protein medium*
  - ___ *Coarse*
  - ___ *High-protein coarse*
  - ___ *Special medium/coarse*

- ☐ HARD WHITE WHOLE-WHEAT
- ☐ BROMATED HIGH-PROTEIN
- ☐ UNBLEACHED ENRICHED
- ☐ BLEACHED WHEAT
- ☐ ARTISAN BREAD
- ☐ IRISH-STYLE WHOLEMEAL
- ☐ HIGH-GLUTEN
- ☐ HIGH-EXTRACTION
  - ___ *Type 70 malted*
  - ___ *Stone ground type 80*
  - ___ *Type 80*
  - ___ *Old country type 85*
  - ___ *Old country type 85 malted*
- ☐ OTHER _____

- ☐ SPECIALTY
  - ___ *Barley*
  - ___ *Coarse cornmeal*
  - ___ *Fine cornmeal*
  - ___ *Polenta*
  - ___ *Flaxseed meal*
  - ___ *Millet*
  - ___ *Brown rice*
  - ___ *White rice*
  - ___ *Cream of rye*
  - ___ *Pumpernickel rye*
  - ___ *White rye*
  - ___ *Whole dark rye*
  - ___ *Spelt*
  - ___ *Semolina*
  - ___ *Whole durum*
  - ___ *Whole-wheat durum*

TYPES OF SALT

- ☐ IODIZED TABLE SALT
- ☐ KOSHER MEDIUM-COARSE SALT
- ☐ PINK HIMALAYAN SALT
- ☐ VOLCANIC BLACK SALT
- ☐ MALDON SALT
- ☐ EXTRA FINE SEA SALT
- ☐ FRENCH GRAY SEA SALT
- ☐ SMOKED SEA SALT
- ☐ SEL GRIS

BAKING CONDITIONS

HUMIDITY

TEMPERATURE

STARTER DESCRIPTION

FINISHED LOAF DESCRIPTION

CRUMB DESCRIPTORS

- ☐ EVEN, "TIGHT" HOLES
- ☐ EVEN, MEDIUM HOLES
- ☐ IRREGULAR, LARGE HOLES
- ☐ DELICATE STRUCTURE
- ☐ AVERAGE STRUCTURE
- ☐ STURDY STRUCTURE
- ☐ TRANSLUCENT
- ☐ DENSE
- ☐ COOL AND CREAMY
- ☐ DRY OR DUSTY
- ☐ OTHER _____

CRUST DESCRIPTORS

- ☐ TENDER, GOLDEN
- ☐ SOFT, COMPRESSIBLE
- ☐ HARD, CRUSTY
- ☐ CARAMELIZED
- ☐ NUTTY
- ☐ BUTTERY
- ☐ OILY
- ☐ TOOTHSOME
- ☐ CRISPY
- ☐ OTHER _____

DATE _____

NOTES

INGREDIENTS

TYPES OF FLOUR

- ☐ ALL-PURPOSE
- ☐ UNBLEACHED ALL-PURPOSE
- ☐ BREAD FLOUR
- ☐ UNBLEACHED WHEAT
  - ___ *Plus malted*
  - ___ *Low ash*
  - ___ *Malted All-purpose*
  - ___ *High-gluten*
- ☐ WHOLE-WHEAT
  - ___ *Fine*
  - ___ *High-protein fine*
  - ___ *Medium*
  - ___ *High-protein medium*
  - ___ *Coarse*
  - ___ *High-protein coarse*
  - ___ *Special medium/coarse*

- ☐ HARD WHITE WHOLE-WHEAT
- ☐ BROMATED HIGH-PROTEIN
- ☐ UNBLEACHED ENRICHED
- ☐ BLEACHED WHEAT
- ☐ ARTISAN BREAD
- ☐ IRISH-STYLE WHOLEMEAL
- ☐ HIGH-GLUTEN
- ☐ HIGH-EXTRACTION
  - ___ *Type 70 malted*
  - ___ *Stone ground type 80*
  - ___ *Type 80*
  - ___ *Old country type 85*
  - ___ *Old country type 85 malted*
- ☐ OTHER _____

- ☐ SPECIALTY
  - ___ *Barley*
  - ___ *Coarse cornmeal*
  - ___ *Fine cornmeal*
  - ___ *Polenta*
  - ___ *Flaxseed meal*
  - ___ *Millet*
  - ___ *Brown rice*
  - ___ *White rice*
  - ___ *Cream of rye*
  - ___ *Pumpernickel rye*
  - ___ *White rye*
  - ___ *Whole dark rye*
  - ___ *Spelt*
  - ___ *Semolina*
  - ___ *Whole durum*
  - ___ *Whole-wheat durum*

TYPES OF SALT

- ☐ IODIZED TABLE SALT
- ☐ KOSHER MEDIUM-COARSE SALT
- ☐ PINK HIMALAYAN SALT
- ☐ VOLCANIC BLACK SALT
- ☐ MALDON SALT
- ☐ EXTRA FINE SEA SALT
- ☐ FRENCH GRAY SEA SALT
- ☐ SMOKED SEA SALT
- ☐ SEL GRIS

BAKING CONDITIONS

HUMIDITY

TEMPERATURE

STARTER DESCRIPTION

FINISHED LOAF DESCRIPTION

CRUMB DESCRIPTORS

- ☐ EVEN, "TIGHT" HOLES
- ☐ EVEN, MEDIUM HOLES
- ☐ IRREGULAR, LARGE HOLES
- ☐ DELICATE STRUCTURE
- ☐ AVERAGE STRUCTURE
- ☐ STURDY STRUCTURE
- ☐ TRANSLUCENT
- ☐ DENSE
- ☐ COOL AND CREAMY
- ☐ DRY OR DUSTY
- ☐ OTHER _____

CRUST DESCRIPTORS

- ☐ TENDER, GOLDEN
- ☐ SOFT, COMPRESSIBLE
- ☐ HARD, CRUSTY
- ☐ CARAMELIZED
- ☐ NUTTY
- ☐ BUTTERY
- ☐ OILY
- ☐ TOOTHSOME
- ☐ CRISPY
- ☐ OTHER _____

DATE _____

INGREDIENTS

TYPES OF FLOUR

- ☐ ALL-PURPOSE
- ☐ UNBLEACHED ALL-PURPOSE
- ☐ BREAD FLOUR
- ☐ UNBLEACHED WHEAT
  - ___ *Plus malted*
  - ___ *Low ash*
  - ___ *Malted All-purpose*
  - ___ *High-gluten*
- ☐ WHOLE-WHEAT
  - ___ *Fine*
  - ___ *High-protein fine*
  - ___ *Medium*
  - ___ *High-protein medium*
  - ___ *Coarse*
  - ___ *High-protein coarse*
  - ___ *Special medium/coarse*

- ☐ HARD WHITE WHOLE-WHEAT
- ☐ BROMATED HIGH-PROTEIN
- ☐ UNBLEACHED ENRICHED
- ☐ BLEACHED WHEAT
- ☐ ARTISAN BREAD
- ☐ IRISH-STYLE WHOLEMEAL
- ☐ HIGH-GLUTEN
- ☐ HIGH-EXTRACTION
  - ___ *Type 70 malted*
  - ___ *Stone ground type 80*
  - ___ *Type 80*
  - ___ *Old country type 85*
  - ___ *Old country type 85 malted*
- ☐ OTHER _____

- ☐ SPECIALTY
  - ___ *Barley*
  - ___ *Coarse cornmeal*
  - ___ *Fine cornmeal*
  - ___ *Polenta*
  - ___ *Flaxseed meal*
  - ___ *Millet*
  - ___ *Brown rice*
  - ___ *White rice*
  - ___ *Cream of rye*
  - ___ *Pumpernickel rye*
  - ___ *White rye*
  - ___ *Whole dark rye*
  - ___ *Spelt*
  - ___ *Semolina*
  - ___ *Whole durum*
  - ___ *Whole-wheat durum*

TYPES OF SALT

- ☐ IODIZED TABLE SALT
- ☐ KOSHER MEDIUM-COARSE SALT
- ☐ PINK HIMALAYAN SALT
- ☐ VOLCANIC BLACK SALT
- ☐ MALDON SALT
- ☐ EXTRA FINE SEA SALT
- ☐ FRENCH GRAY SEA SALT
- ☐ SMOKED SEA SALT
- ☐ SEL GRIS

BAKING CONDITIONS

HUMIDITY

TEMPERATURE

STARTER DESCRIPTION

FINISHED LOAF DESCRIPTION

CRUMB DESCRIPTORS

- ☐ EVEN, "TIGHT" HOLES
- ☐ EVEN, MEDIUM HOLES
- ☐ IRREGULAR, LARGE HOLES
- ☐ DELICATE STRUCTURE
- ☐ AVERAGE STRUCTURE
- ☐ STURDY STRUCTURE
- ☐ TRANSLUCENT
- ☐ DENSE
- ☐ COOL AND CREAMY
- ☐ DRY OR DUSTY
- ☐ OTHER _____

CRUST DESCRIPTORS

- ☐ TENDER, GOLDEN
- ☐ SOFT, COMPRESSIBLE
- ☐ HARD, CRUSTY
- ☐ CARAMELIZED
- ☐ NUTTY
- ☐ BUTTERY
- ☐ OILY
- ☐ TOOTHSOME
- ☐ CRISPY
- ☐ OTHER _____

DATE _____

INGREDIENTS

TYPES OF FLOUR

- ☐ ALL-PURPOSE
- ☐ UNBLEACHED ALL-PURPOSE
- ☐ BREAD FLOUR
- ☐ UNBLEACHED WHEAT
  - ___ *Plus malted*
  - ___ *Low ash*
  - ___ *Malted All-purpose*
  - ___ *High-gluten*
- ☐ WHOLE-WHEAT
  - ___ *Fine*
  - ___ *High-protein fine*
  - ___ *Medium*
  - ___ *High-protein medium*
  - ___ *Coarse*
  - ___ *High-protein coarse*
  - ___ *Special medium/coarse*

- ☐ HARD WHITE WHOLE-WHEAT
- ☐ BROMATED HIGH-PROTEIN
- ☐ UNBLEACHED ENRICHED
- ☐ BLEACHED WHEAT
- ☐ ARTISAN BREAD
- ☐ IRISH-STYLE WHOLEMEAL
- ☐ HIGH-GLUTEN
- ☐ HIGH-EXTRACTION
  - ___ *Type 70 malted*
  - ___ *Stone ground type 80*
  - ___ *Type 80*
  - ___ *Old country type 85*
  - ___ *Old country type 85 malted*
- ☐ OTHER _____

- ☐ SPECIALTY
  - ___ *Barley*
  - ___ *Coarse cornmeal*
  - ___ *Fine cornmeal*
  - ___ *Polenta*
  - ___ *Flaxseed meal*
  - ___ *Millet*
  - ___ *Brown rice*
  - ___ *White rice*
  - ___ *Cream of rye*
  - ___ *Pumpernickel rye*
  - ___ *White rye*
  - ___ *Whole dark rye*
  - ___ *Spelt*
  - ___ *Semolina*
  - ___ *Whole durum*
  - ___ *Whole-wheat durum*

TYPES OF SALT

- ☐ IODIZED TABLE SALT
- ☐ KOSHER MEDIUM-COARSE SALT
- ☐ PINK HIMALAYAN SALT
- ☐ VOLCANIC BLACK SALT
- ☐ MALDON SALT
- ☐ EXTRA FINE SEA SALT
- ☐ FRENCH GRAY SEA SALT
- ☐ SMOKED SEA SALT
- ☐ SEL GRIS

BAKING CONDITIONS

HUMIDITY

TEMPERATURE

STARTER DESCRIPTION

FINISHED LOAF DESCRIPTION

CRUMB DESCRIPTORS

- ☐ EVEN, "TIGHT" HOLES
- ☐ EVEN, MEDIUM HOLES
- ☐ IRREGULAR, LARGE HOLES
- ☐ DELICATE STRUCTURE
- ☐ AVERAGE STRUCTURE
- ☐ STURDY STRUCTURE
- ☐ TRANSLUCENT
- ☐ DENSE
- ☐ COOL AND CREAMY
- ☐ DRY OR DUSTY
- ☐ OTHER _____

CRUST DESCRIPTORS

- ☐ TENDER, GOLDEN
- ☐ SOFT, COMPRESSIBLE
- ☐ HARD, CRUSTY
- ☐ CARAMELIZED
- ☐ NUTTY
- ☐ BUTTERY
- ☐ OILY
- ☐ TOOTHSOME
- ☐ CRISPY
- ☐ OTHER _____

DATE _____

INGREDIENTS

TYPES OF FLOUR

- ☐ ALL-PURPOSE
- ☐ UNBLEACHED ALL-PURPOSE
- ☐ BREAD FLOUR
- ☐ UNBLEACHED WHEAT
  - ___ *Plus malted*
  - ___ *Low ash*
  - ___ *Malted All-purpose*
  - ___ *High-gluten*
- ☐ WHOLE-WHEAT
  - ___ *Fine*
  - ___ *High-protein fine*
  - ___ *Medium*
  - ___ *High-protein medium*
  - ___ *Coarse*
  - ___ *High-protein coarse*
  - ___ *Special medium/coarse*

- ☐ HARD WHITE WHOLE-WHEAT
- ☐ BROMATED HIGH-PROTEIN
- ☐ UNBLEACHED ENRICHED
- ☐ BLEACHED WHEAT
- ☐ ARTISAN BREAD
- ☐ IRISH-STYLE WHOLEMEAL
- ☐ HIGH-GLUTEN
- ☐ HIGH-EXTRACTION
  - ___ *Type 70 malted*
  - ___ *Stone ground type 80*
  - ___ *Type 80*
  - ___ *Old country type 85*
  - ___ *Old country type 85 malted*
- ☐ OTHER _____

- ☐ SPECIALTY
  - ___ *Barley*
  - ___ *Coarse cornmeal*
  - ___ *Fine cornmeal*
  - ___ *Polenta*
  - ___ *Flaxseed meal*
  - ___ *Millet*
  - ___ *Brown rice*
  - ___ *White rice*
  - ___ *Cream of rye*
  - ___ *Pumpernickel rye*
  - ___ *White rye*
  - ___ *Whole dark rye*
  - ___ *Spelt*
  - ___ *Semolina*
  - ___ *Whole durum*
  - ___ *Whole-wheat durum*

TYPES OF SALT

- ☐ IODIZED TABLE SALT
- ☐ KOSHER MEDIUM-COARSE SALT
- ☐ PINK HIMALAYAN SALT
- ☐ VOLCANIC BLACK SALT
- ☐ MALDON SALT
- ☐ EXTRA FINE SEA SALT
- ☐ FRENCH GRAY SEA SALT
- ☐ SMOKED SEA SALT
- ☐ SEL GRIS

BAKING CONDITIONS

HUMIDITY

TEMPERATURE

STARTER DESCRIPTION

FINISHED LOAF DESCRIPTION

CRUMB DESCRIPTORS

- ☐ EVEN, "TIGHT" HOLES
- ☐ EVEN, MEDIUM HOLES
- ☐ IRREGULAR, LARGE HOLES
- ☐ DELICATE STRUCTURE
- ☐ AVERAGE STRUCTURE
- ☐ STURDY STRUCTURE
- ☐ TRANSLUCENT
- ☐ DENSE
- ☐ COOL AND CREAMY
- ☐ DRY OR DUSTY
- ☐ OTHER _____

CRUST DESCRIPTORS

- ☐ TENDER, GOLDEN
- ☐ SOFT, COMPRESSIBLE
- ☐ HARD, CRUSTY
- ☐ CARAMELIZED
- ☐ NUTTY
- ☐ BUTTERY
- ☐ OILY
- ☐ TOOTHSOME
- ☐ CRISPY
- ☐ OTHER _____

DATE _____

NOTES

INGREDIENTS

TYPES OF FLOUR

- ☐ ALL-PURPOSE
- ☐ UNBLEACHED ALL-PURPOSE
- ☐ BREAD FLOUR
- ☐ UNBLEACHED WHEAT
  - ___ *Plus malted*
  - ___ *Low ash*
  - ___ *Malted All-purpose*
  - ___ *High-gluten*
- ☐ WHOLE-WHEAT
  - ___ *Fine*
  - ___ *High-protein fine*
  - ___ *Medium*
  - ___ *High-protein medium*
  - ___ *Coarse*
  - ___ *High-protein coarse*
  - ___ *Special medium/coarse*

- ☐ HARD WHITE WHOLE-WHEAT
- ☐ BROMATED HIGH-PROTEIN
- ☐ UNBLEACHED ENRICHED
- ☐ BLEACHED WHEAT
- ☐ ARTISAN BREAD
- ☐ IRISH-STYLE WHOLEMEAL
- ☐ HIGH-GLUTEN
- ☐ HIGH-EXTRACTION
  - ___ *Type 70 malted*
  - ___ *Stone ground type 80*
  - ___ *Type 80*
  - ___ *Old country type 85*
  - ___ *Old country type 85 malted*
- ☐ OTHER _____

- ☐ SPECIALTY
  - ___ *Barley*
  - ___ *Coarse cornmeal*
  - ___ *Fine cornmeal*
  - ___ *Polenta*
  - ___ *Flaxseed meal*
  - ___ *Millet*
  - ___ *Brown rice*
  - ___ *White rice*
  - ___ *Cream of rye*
  - ___ *Pumpernickel rye*
  - ___ *White rye*
  - ___ *Whole dark rye*
  - ___ *Spelt*
  - ___ *Semolina*
  - ___ *Whole durum*
  - ___ *Whole-wheat durum*

TYPES OF SALT

- ☐ IODIZED TABLE SALT
- ☐ KOSHER MEDIUM-COARSE SALT
- ☐ PINK HIMALAYAN SALT
- ☐ VOLCANIC BLACK SALT
- ☐ MALDON SALT
- ☐ EXTRA FINE SEA SALT
- ☐ FRENCH GRAY SEA SALT
- ☐ SMOKED SEA SALT
- ☐ SEL GRIS

BAKING CONDITIONS

HUMIDITY

TEMPERATURE

STARTER DESCRIPTION

FINISHED LOAF DESCRIPTION

CRUMB DESCRIPTORS

- ☐ EVEN, "TIGHT" HOLES
- ☐ EVEN, MEDIUM HOLES
- ☐ IRREGULAR, LARGE HOLES
- ☐ DELICATE STRUCTURE
- ☐ AVERAGE STRUCTURE
- ☐ STURDY STRUCTURE
- ☐ TRANSLUCENT
- ☐ DENSE
- ☐ COOL AND CREAMY
- ☐ DRY OR DUSTY
- ☐ OTHER _____

CRUST DESCRIPTORS

- ☐ TENDER, GOLDEN
- ☐ SOFT, COMPRESSIBLE
- ☐ HARD, CRUSTY
- ☐ CARAMELIZED
- ☐ NUTTY
- ☐ BUTTERY
- ☐ OILY
- ☐ TOOTHSOME
- ☐ CRISPY
- ☐ OTHER _____

DATE _____

NOTES

INGREDIENTS

TYPES OF FLOUR

☐ ALL-PURPOSE
☐ UNBLEACHED ALL-PURPOSE
☐ BREAD FLOUR
☐ UNBLEACHED WHEAT
  ___ *Plus malted*
  ___ *Low ash*
  ___ *Malted All-purpose*
  ___ *High-gluten*
☐ WHOLE-WHEAT
  ___ *Fine*
  ___ *High-protein fine*
  ___ *Medium*
  ___ *High-protein medium*
  ___ *Coarse*
  ___ *High-protein coarse*
  ___ *Special medium/coarse*

☐ HARD WHITE WHOLE-WHEAT
☐ BROMATED HIGH-PROTEIN
☐ UNBLEACHED ENRICHED
☐ BLEACHED WHEAT
☐ ARTISAN BREAD
☐ IRISH-STYLE WHOLEMEAL
☐ HIGH-GLUTEN
☐ HIGH-EXTRACTION
  ___ *Type 70 malted*
  ___ *Stone ground type 80*
  ___ *Type 80*
  ___ *Old country type 85*
  ___ *Old country type 85 malted*
☐ OTHER _____

☐ SPECIALTY
  ___ *Barley*
  ___ *Coarse cornmeal*
  ___ *Fine cornmeal*
  ___ *Polenta*
  ___ *Flaxseed meal*
  ___ *Millet*
  ___ *Brown rice*
  ___ *White rice*
  ___ *Cream of rye*
  ___ *Pumpernickel rye*
  ___ *White rye*
  ___ *Whole dark rye*
  ___ *Spelt*
  ___ *Semolina*
  ___ *Whole durum*
  ___ *Whole-wheat durum*

TYPES OF SALT

☐ IODIZED TABLE SALT
☐ KOSHER MEDIUM-COARSE SALT
☐ PINK HIMALAYAN SALT
☐ VOLCANIC BLACK SALT
☐ MALDON SALT
☐ EXTRA FINE SEA SALT
☐ FRENCH GRAY SEA SALT
☐ SMOKED SEA SALT
☐ SEL GRIS

BAKING CONDITIONS

HUMIDITY

TEMPERATURE

STARTER DESCRIPTION

FINISHED LOAF DESCRIPTION

CRUMB DESCRIPTORS

☐ EVEN, "TIGHT" HOLES
☐ EVEN, MEDIUM HOLES
☐ IRREGULAR, LARGE HOLES
☐ DELICATE STRUCTURE
☐ AVERAGE STRUCTURE
☐ STURDY STRUCTURE
☐ TRANSLUCENT
☐ DENSE
☐ COOL AND CREAMY
☐ DRY OR DUSTY
☐ OTHER _____

CRUST DESCRIPTORS

☐ TENDER, GOLDEN
☐ SOFT, COMPRESSIBLE
☐ HARD, CRUSTY
☐ CARAMELIZED
☐ NUTTY
☐ BUTTERY
☐ OILY
☐ TOOTHSOME
☐ CRISPY
☐ OTHER _____

DATE _____

NOTES

INGREDIENTS

TYPES OF FLOUR

- ☐ ALL-PURPOSE
- ☐ UNBLEACHED ALL-PURPOSE
- ☐ BREAD FLOUR
- ☐ UNBLEACHED WHEAT
  - ___ *Plus malted*
  - ___ *Low ash*
  - ___ *Malted All-purpose*
  - ___ *High-gluten*
- ☐ WHOLE-WHEAT
  - ___ *Fine*
  - ___ *High-protein fine*
  - ___ *Medium*
  - ___ *High-protein medium*
  - ___ *Coarse*
  - ___ *High-protein coarse*
  - ___ *Special medium/coarse*

- ☐ HARD WHITE WHOLE-WHEAT
- ☐ BROMATED HIGH-PROTEIN
- ☐ UNBLEACHED ENRICHED
- ☐ BLEACHED WHEAT
- ☐ ARTISAN BREAD
- ☐ IRISH-STYLE WHOLEMEAL
- ☐ HIGH-GLUTEN
- ☐ HIGH-EXTRACTION
  - ___ *Type 70 malted*
  - ___ *Stone ground type 80*
  - ___ *Type 80*
  - ___ *Old country type 85*
  - ___ *Old country type 85 malted*
- ☐ OTHER _____

- ☐ SPECIALTY
  - ___ *Barley*
  - ___ *Coarse cornmeal*
  - ___ *Fine cornmeal*
  - ___ *Polenta*
  - ___ *Flaxseed meal*
  - ___ *Millet*
  - ___ *Brown rice*
  - ___ *White rice*
  - ___ *Cream of rye*
  - ___ *Pumpernickel rye*
  - ___ *White rye*
  - ___ *Whole dark rye*
  - ___ *Spelt*
  - ___ *Semolina*
  - ___ *Whole durum*
  - ___ *Whole-wheat durum*

TYPES OF SALT

- ☐ IODIZED TABLE SALT
- ☐ KOSHER MEDIUM-COARSE SALT
- ☐ PINK HIMALAYAN SALT
- ☐ VOLCANIC BLACK SALT
- ☐ MALDON SALT
- ☐ EXTRA FINE SEA SALT
- ☐ FRENCH GRAY SEA SALT
- ☐ SMOKED SEA SALT
- ☐ SEL GRIS

BAKING CONDITIONS

HUMIDITY

TEMPERATURE

STARTER DESCRIPTION

FINISHED LOAF DESCRIPTION

CRUMB DESCRIPTORS

- ☐ EVEN, "TIGHT" HOLES
- ☐ EVEN, MEDIUM HOLES
- ☐ IRREGULAR, LARGE HOLES
- ☐ DELICATE STRUCTURE
- ☐ AVERAGE STRUCTURE
- ☐ STURDY STRUCTURE
- ☐ TRANSLUCENT
- ☐ DENSE
- ☐ COOL AND CREAMY
- ☐ DRY OR DUSTY
- ☐ OTHER _____

CRUST DESCRIPTORS

- ☐ TENDER, GOLDEN
- ☐ SOFT, COMPRESSIBLE
- ☐ HARD, CRUSTY
- ☐ CARAMELIZED
- ☐ NUTTY
- ☐ BUTTERY
- ☐ OILY
- ☐ TOOTHSOME
- ☐ CRISPY
- ☐ OTHER _____

DATE _____

NOTES

INGREDIENTS

TYPES OF FLOUR

- ☐ ALL-PURPOSE
- ☐ UNBLEACHED ALL-PURPOSE
- ☐ BREAD FLOUR
- ☐ UNBLEACHED WHEAT
  - ___ *Plus malted*
  - ___ *Low ash*
  - ___ *Malted All-purpose*
  - ___ *High-gluten*
- ☐ WHOLE-WHEAT
  - ___ *Fine*
  - ___ *High-protein fine*
  - ___ *Medium*
  - ___ *High-protein medium*
  - ___ *Coarse*
  - ___ *High-protein coarse*
  - ___ *Special medium/coarse*

- ☐ HARD WHITE WHOLE-WHEAT
- ☐ BROMATED HIGH-PROTEIN
- ☐ UNBLEACHED ENRICHED
- ☐ BLEACHED WHEAT
- ☐ ARTISAN BREAD
- ☐ IRISH-STYLE WHOLEMEAL
- ☐ HIGH-GLUTEN
- ☐ HIGH-EXTRACTION
  - ___ *Type 70 malted*
  - ___ *Stone ground type 80*
  - ___ *Type 80*
  - ___ *Old country type 85*
  - ___ *Old country type 85 malted*
- ☐ OTHER _____

- ☐ SPECIALTY
  - ___ *Barley*
  - ___ *Coarse cornmeal*
  - ___ *Fine cornmeal*
  - ___ *Polenta*
  - ___ *Flaxseed meal*
  - ___ *Millet*
  - ___ *Brown rice*
  - ___ *White rice*
  - ___ *Cream of rye*
  - ___ *Pumpernickel rye*
  - ___ *White rye*
  - ___ *Whole dark rye*
  - ___ *Spelt*
  - ___ *Semolina*
  - ___ *Whole durum*
  - ___ *Whole-wheat durum*

TYPES OF SALT

- ☐ IODIZED TABLE SALT
- ☐ KOSHER MEDIUM-COARSE SALT
- ☐ PINK HIMALAYAN SALT
- ☐ VOLCANIC BLACK SALT
- ☐ MALDON SALT
- ☐ EXTRA FINE SEA SALT
- ☐ FRENCH GRAY SEA SALT
- ☐ SMOKED SEA SALT
- ☐ SEL GRIS

BAKING CONDITIONS

HUMIDITY

TEMPERATURE

STARTER DESCRIPTION

FINISHED LOAF DESCRIPTION

CRUMB DESCRIPTORS

- ☐ EVEN, "TIGHT" HOLES
- ☐ EVEN, MEDIUM HOLES
- ☐ IRREGULAR, LARGE HOLES
- ☐ DELICATE STRUCTURE
- ☐ AVERAGE STRUCTURE
- ☐ STURDY STRUCTURE
- ☐ TRANSLUCENT
- ☐ DENSE
- ☐ COOL AND CREAMY
- ☐ DRY OR DUSTY
- ☐ OTHER _____

CRUST DESCRIPTORS

- ☐ TENDER, GOLDEN
- ☐ SOFT, COMPRESSIBLE
- ☐ HARD, CRUSTY
- ☐ CARAMELIZED
- ☐ NUTTY
- ☐ BUTTERY
- ☐ OILY
- ☐ TOOTHSOME
- ☐ CRISPY
- ☐ OTHER _____

DATE _____

INGREDIENTS

TYPES OF FLOUR

- ☐ ALL-PURPOSE
- ☐ UNBLEACHED ALL-PURPOSE
- ☐ BREAD FLOUR
- ☐ UNBLEACHED WHEAT
  - ___ *Plus malted*
  - ___ *Low ash*
  - ___ *Malted All-purpose*
  - ___ *High-gluten*
- ☐ WHOLE-WHEAT
  - ___ *Fine*
  - ___ *High-protein fine*
  - ___ *Medium*
  - ___ *High-protein medium*
  - ___ *Coarse*
  - ___ *High-protein coarse*
  - ___ *Special medium/coarse*

- ☐ HARD WHITE WHOLE-WHEAT
- ☐ BROMATED HIGH-PROTEIN
- ☐ UNBLEACHED ENRICHED
- ☐ BLEACHED WHEAT
- ☐ ARTISAN BREAD
- ☐ IRISH-STYLE WHOLEMEAL
- ☐ HIGH-GLUTEN
- ☐ HIGH-EXTRACTION
  - ___ *Type 70 malted*
  - ___ *Stone ground type 80*
  - ___ *Type 80*
  - ___ *Old country type 85*
  - ___ *Old country type 85 malted*
- ☐ OTHER _____

- ☐ SPECIALTY
  - ___ *Barley*
  - ___ *Coarse cornmeal*
  - ___ *Fine cornmeal*
  - ___ *Polenta*
  - ___ *Flaxseed meal*
  - ___ *Millet*
  - ___ *Brown rice*
  - ___ *White rice*
  - ___ *Cream of rye*
  - ___ *Pumpernickel rye*
  - ___ *White rye*
  - ___ *Whole dark rye*
  - ___ *Spelt*
  - ___ *Semolina*
  - ___ *Whole durum*
  - ___ *Whole-wheat durum*

TYPES OF SALT

- ☐ IODIZED TABLE SALT
- ☐ KOSHER MEDIUM-COARSE SALT
- ☐ PINK HIMALAYAN SALT
- ☐ VOLCANIC BLACK SALT
- ☐ MALDON SALT
- ☐ EXTRA FINE SEA SALT
- ☐ FRENCH GRAY SEA SALT
- ☐ SMOKED SEA SALT
- ☐ SEL GRIS

BAKING CONDITIONS

HUMIDITY

TEMPERATURE

STARTER DESCRIPTION

FINISHED LOAF DESCRIPTION

CRUMB DESCRIPTORS

- ☐ EVEN, "TIGHT" HOLES
- ☐ EVEN, MEDIUM HOLES
- ☐ IRREGULAR, LARGE HOLES
- ☐ DELICATE STRUCTURE
- ☐ AVERAGE STRUCTURE
- ☐ STURDY STRUCTURE
- ☐ TRANSLUCENT
- ☐ DENSE
- ☐ COOL AND CREAMY
- ☐ DRY OR DUSTY
- ☐ OTHER _____

CRUST DESCRIPTORS

- ☐ TENDER, GOLDEN
- ☐ SOFT, COMPRESSIBLE
- ☐ HARD, CRUSTY
- ☐ CARAMELIZED
- ☐ NUTTY
- ☐ BUTTERY
- ☐ OILY
- ☐ TOOTHSOME
- ☐ CRISPY
- ☐ OTHER _____

DATE _____

NOTES

INGREDIENTS

TYPES OF FLOUR

- ☐ ALL-PURPOSE
- ☐ UNBLEACHED ALL-PURPOSE
- ☐ BREAD FLOUR
- ☐ UNBLEACHED WHEAT
  - ___ *Plus malted*
  - ___ *Low ash*
  - ___ *Malted All-purpose*
  - ___ *High-gluten*
- ☐ WHOLE-WHEAT
  - ___ *Fine*
  - ___ *High protein fine*
  - ___ *Medium*
  - ___ *High-protein medium*
  - ___ *Coarse*
  - ___ *High-protein coarse*
  - ___ *Special medium/coarse*

- ☐ HARD WHITE WHOLE-WHEAT
- ☐ BROMATED HIGH-PROTEIN
- ☐ UNBLEACHED ENRICHED
- ☐ BLEACHED WHEAT
- ☐ ARTISAN BREAD
- ☐ IRISH-STYLE WHOLEMEAL
- ☐ HIGH-GLUTEN
- ☐ HIGH-EXTRACTION
  - ___ *Type 70 malted*
  - ___ *Stone ground type 80*
  - ___ *Type 80*
  - ___ *Old country type 85*
  - ___ *Old country type 85 malted*
- ☐ OTHER _____

- ☐ SPECIALTY
  - ___ *Barley*
  - ___ *Coarse cornmeal*
  - ___ *Fine cornmeal*
  - ___ *Polenta*
  - ___ *Flaxseed meal*
  - ___ *Millet*
  - ___ *Brown rice*
  - ___ *White rice*
  - ___ *Cream of rye*
  - ___ *Pumpernickel rye*
  - ___ *White rye*
  - ___ *Whole dark rye*
  - ___ *Spelt*
  - ___ *Semolina*
  - ___ *Whole durum*
  - ___ *Whole-wheat durum*

TYPES OF SALT

- ☐ IODIZED TABLE SALT
- ☐ KOSHER MEDIUM-COARSE SALT
- ☐ PINK HIMALAYAN SALT
- ☐ VOLCANIC BLACK SALT
- ☐ MALDON SALT
- ☐ EXTRA FINE SEA SALT
- ☐ FRENCH GRAY SEA SALT
- ☐ SMOKED SEA SALT
- ☐ SEL GRIS

BAKING CONDITIONS

HUMIDITY

TEMPERATURE

STARTER DESCRIPTION

FINISHED LOAF DESCRIPTION

CRUMB DESCRIPTORS

- ☐ EVEN, "TIGHT" HOLES
- ☐ EVEN, MEDIUM HOLES
- ☐ IRREGULAR, LARGE HOLES
- ☐ DELICATE STRUCTURE
- ☐ AVERAGE STRUCTURE
- ☐ STURDY STRUCTURE
- ☐ TRANSLUCENT
- ☐ DENSE
- ☐ COOL AND CREAMY
- ☐ DRY OR DUSTY
- ☐ OTHER _____

CRUST DESCRIPTORS

- ☐ TENDER, GOLDEN
- ☐ SOFT, COMPRESSIBLE
- ☐ HARD, CRUSTY
- ☐ CARAMELIZED
- ☐ NUTTY
- ☐ BUTTERY
- ☐ OILY
- ☐ TOOTHSOME
- ☐ CRISPY
- ☐ OTHER _____

DATE _____

INGREDIENTS

TYPES OF FLOUR

- ☐ ALL-PURPOSE
- ☐ UNBLEACHED ALL-PURPOSE
- ☐ BREAD FLOUR
- ☐ UNBLEACHED WHEAT
  - ___ *Plus malted*
  - ___ *Low ash*
  - ___ *Malted All-purpose*
  - ___ *High-gluten*
- ☐ WHOLE-WHEAT
  - ___ *Fine*
  - ___ *High-protein fine*
  - ___ *Medium*
  - ___ *High-protein medium*
  - ___ *Coarse*
  - ___ *High-protein coarse*
  - ___ *Special medium/coarse*

- ☐ HARD WHITE WHOLE-WHEAT
- ☐ BROMATED HIGH-PROTEIN
- ☐ UNBLEACHED ENRICHED
- ☐ BLEACHED WHEAT
- ☐ ARTISAN BREAD
- ☐ IRISH-STYLE WHOLEMEAL
- ☐ HIGH-GLUTEN
- ☐ HIGH-EXTRACTION
  - ___ *Type 70 malted*
  - ___ *Stone ground type 80*
  - ___ *Type 80*
  - ___ *Old country type 85*
  - ___ *Old country type 85 malted*
- ☐ OTHER _____

- ☐ SPECIALTY
  - ___ *Barley*
  - ___ *Coarse cornmeal*
  - ___ *Fine cornmeal*
  - ___ *Polenta*
  - ___ *Flaxseed meal*
  - ___ *Millet*
  - ___ *Brown rice*
  - ___ *White rice*
  - ___ *Cream of rye*
  - ___ *Pumpernickel rye*
  - ___ *White rye*
  - ___ *Whole dark rye*
  - ___ *Spelt*
  - ___ *Semolina*
  - ___ *Whole durum*
  - ___ *Whole-wheat durum*

TYPES OF SALT

- ☐ IODIZED TABLE SALT
- ☐ KOSHER MEDIUM-COARSE SALT
- ☐ PINK HIMALAYAN SALT
- ☐ VOLCANIC BLACK SALT
- ☐ MALDON SALT
- ☐ EXTRA FINE SEA SALT
- ☐ FRENCH GRAY SEA SALT
- ☐ SMOKED SEA SALT
- ☐ SEL GRIS

BAKING CONDITIONS

HUMIDITY

TEMPERATURE

STARTER DESCRIPTION

FINISHED LOAF DESCRIPTION

CRUMB DESCRIPTORS

- ☐ EVEN, "TIGHT" HOLES
- ☐ EVEN, MEDIUM HOLES
- ☐ IRREGULAR, LARGE HOLES
- ☐ DELICATE STRUCTURE
- ☐ AVERAGE STRUCTURE
- ☐ STURDY STRUCTURE
- ☐ TRANSLUCENT
- ☐ DENSE
- ☐ COOL AND CREAMY
- ☐ DRY OR DUSTY
- ☐ OTHER _____

CRUST DESCRIPTORS

- ☐ TENDER, GOLDEN
- ☐ SOFT, COMPRESSIBLE
- ☐ HARD, CRUSTY
- ☐ CARAMELIZED
- ☐ NUTTY
- ☐ BUTTERY
- ☐ OILY
- ☐ TOOTHSOME
- ☐ CRISPY
- ☐ OTHER _____

DATE _____

INGREDIENTS

TYPES OF FLOUR

- ☐ ALL-PURPOSE
- ☐ UNBLEACHED ALL-PURPOSE
- ☐ BREAD FLOUR
- ☐ UNBLEACHED WHEAT
  - ___ *Plus malted*
  - ___ *Low ash*
  - ___ *Malted All-purpose*
  - ___ *High-gluten*
- ☐ WHOLE-WHEAT
  - ___ *Fine*
  - ___ *High-protein fine*
  - ___ *Medium*
  - ___ *High-protein medium*
  - ___ *Coarse*
  - ___ *High-protein coarse*
  - ___ *Special medium/coarse*

- ☐ HARD WHITE WHOLE-WHEAT
- ☐ BROMATED HIGH-PROTEIN
- ☐ UNBLEACHED ENRICHED
- ☐ BLEACHED WHEAT
- ☐ ARTISAN BREAD
- ☐ IRISH-STYLE WHOLEMEAL
- ☐ HIGH-GLUTEN
- ☐ HIGH-EXTRACTION
  - ___ *Type 70 malted*
  - ___ *Stone ground type 80*
  - ___ *Type 80*
  - ___ *Old country type 85*
  - ___ *Old country type 85 malted*
- ☐ OTHER _____

- ☐ SPECIALTY
  - ___ *Barley*
  - ___ *Coarse cornmeal*
  - ___ *Fine cornmeal*
  - ___ *Polenta*
  - ___ *Flaxseed meal*
  - ___ *Millet*
  - ___ *Brown rice*
  - ___ *White rice*
  - ___ *Cream of rye*
  - ___ *Pumpernickel rye*
  - ___ *White rye*
  - ___ *Whole dark rye*
  - ___ *Spelt*
  - ___ *Semolina*
  - ___ *Whole durum*
  - ___ *Whole-wheat durum*

TYPES OF SALT

- ☐ IODIZED TABLE SALT
- ☐ KOSHER MEDIUM-COARSE SALT
- ☐ PINK HIMALAYAN SALT
- ☐ VOLCANIC BLACK SALT
- ☐ MALDON SALT
- ☐ EXTRA FINE SEA SALT
- ☐ FRENCH GRAY SEA SALT
- ☐ SMOKED SEA SALT
- ☐ SEL GRIS

BAKING CONDITIONS

HUMIDITY

TEMPERATURE

STARTER DESCRIPTION

FINISHED LOAF DESCRIPTION

CRUMB DESCRIPTORS

- ☐ EVEN, "TIGHT" HOLES
- ☐ EVEN, MEDIUM HOLES
- ☐ IRREGULAR, LARGE HOLES
- ☐ DELICATE STRUCTURE
- ☐ AVERAGE STRUCTURE
- ☐ STURDY STRUCTURE
- ☐ TRANSLUCENT
- ☐ DENSE
- ☐ COOL AND CREAMY
- ☐ DRY OR DUSTY
- ☐ OTHER _____

CRUST DESCRIPTORS

- ☐ TENDER, GOLDEN
- ☐ SOFT, COMPRESSIBLE
- ☐ HARD, CRUSTY
- ☐ CARAMELIZED
- ☐ NUTTY
- ☐ BUTTERY
- ☐ OILY
- ☐ TOOTHSOME
- ☐ CRISPY
- ☐ OTHER _____

DATE _____

NOTES

INGREDIENTS

TYPES OF FLOUR

- ☐ ALL-PURPOSE
- ☐ UNBLEACHED ALL-PURPOSE
- ☐ BREAD FLOUR
- ☐ UNBLEACHED WHEAT
  - ___ *Plus malted*
  - ___ *Low ash*
  - ___ *Malted All-purpose*
  - ___ *High-gluten*
- ☐ WHOLE-WHEAT
  - ___ *Fine*
  - ___ *High-protein fine*
  - ___ *Medium*
  - ___ *High-protein medium*
  - ___ *Coarse*
  - ___ *High-protein coarse*
  - ___ *Special medium/coarse*

- ☐ HARD WHITE WHOLE-WHEAT
- ☐ BROMATED HIGH-PROTEIN
- ☐ UNBLEACHED ENRICHED
- ☐ BLEACHED WHEAT
- ☐ ARTISAN BREAD
- ☐ IRISH-STYLE WHOLEMEAL
- ☐ HIGH-GLUTEN
- ☐ HIGH-EXTRACTION
  - ___ *Type 70 malted*
  - ___ *Stone ground type 80*
  - ___ *Type 80*
  - ___ *Old country type 85*
  - ___ *Old country type 85 malted*
- ☐ OTHER _____

- ☐ SPECIALTY
  - ___ *Barley*
  - ___ *Coarse cornmeal*
  - ___ *Fine cornmeal*
  - ___ *Polenta*
  - ___ *Flaxseed meal*
  - ___ *Millet*
  - ___ *Brown rice*
  - ___ *White rice*
  - ___ *Cream of rye*
  - ___ *Pumpernickel rye*
  - ___ *White rye*
  - ___ *Whole dark rye*
  - ___ *Spelt*
  - ___ *Semolina*
  - ___ *Whole durum*
  - ___ *Whole-wheat durum*

TYPES OF SALT

- ☐ IODIZED TABLE SALT
- ☐ KOSHER MEDIUM-COARSE SALT
- ☐ PINK HIMALAYAN SALT
- ☐ VOLCANIC BLACK SALT
- ☐ MALDON SALT
- ☐ EXTRA FINE SEA SALT
- ☐ FRENCH GRAY SEA SALT
- ☐ SMOKED SEA SALT
- ☐ SEL GRIS

BAKING CONDITIONS

HUMIDITY

TEMPERATURE

STARTER DESCRIPTION

FINISHED LOAF DESCRIPTION

CRUMB DESCRIPTORS

- ☐ EVEN, "TIGHT" HOLES
- ☐ EVEN, MEDIUM HOLES
- ☐ IRREGULAR, LARGE HOLES
- ☐ DELICATE STRUCTURE
- ☐ AVERAGE STRUCTURE
- ☐ STURDY STRUCTURE
- ☐ TRANSLUCENT
- ☐ DENSE
- ☐ COOL AND CREAMY
- ☐ DRY OR DUSTY
- ☐ OTHER _____

CRUST DESCRIPTORS

- ☐ TENDER, GOLDEN
- ☐ SOFT, COMPRESSIBLE
- ☐ HARD, CRUSTY
- ☐ CARAMELIZED
- ☐ NUTTY
- ☐ BUTTERY
- ☐ OILY
- ☐ TOOTHSOME
- ☐ CRISPY
- ☐ OTHER _____

DATE _____

INGREDIENTS

TYPES OF FLOUR

- [ ] ALL-PURPOSE
- [ ] UNBLEACHED ALL-PURPOSE
- [ ] BREAD FLOUR
- [ ] UNBLEACHED WHEAT
  - ___ *Plus malted*
  - ___ *Low ash*
  - ___ *Malted All-purpose*
  - ___ *High-gluten*
- [ ] WHOLE-WHEAT
  - ___ *Fine*
  - ___ *High-protein fine*
  - ___ *Medium*
  - ___ *High-protein medium*
  - ___ *Coarse*
  - ___ *High-protein coarse*
  - ___ *Special medium/coarse*

- [ ] HARD WHITE WHOLE-WHEAT
- [ ] BROMATED HIGH-PROTEIN
- [ ] UNBLEACHED ENRICHED
- [ ] BLEACHED WHEAT
- [ ] ARTISAN BREAD
- [ ] IRISH-STYLE WHOLEMEAL
- [ ] HIGH-GLUTEN
- [ ] HIGH-EXTRACTION
  - ___ *Type 70 malted*
  - ___ *Stone ground type 80*
  - ___ *Type 80*
  - ___ *Old country type 85*
  - ___ *Old country type 85 malted*
- [ ] OTHER _____

- [ ] SPECIALTY
  - ___ *Barley*
  - ___ *Coarse cornmeal*
  - ___ *Fine cornmeal*
  - ___ *Polenta*
  - ___ *Flaxseed meal*
  - ___ *Millet*
  - ___ *Brown rice*
  - ___ *White rice*
  - ___ *Cream of rye*
  - ___ *Pumpernickel rye*
  - ___ *White rye*
  - ___ *Whole dark rye*
  - ___ *Spelt*
  - ___ *Semolina*
  - ___ *Whole durum*
  - ___ *Whole-wheat durum*

TYPES OF SALT

- [ ] IODIZED TABLE SALT
- [ ] KOSHER MEDIUM-COARSE SALT
- [ ] PINK HIMALAYAN SALT
- [ ] VOLCANIC BLACK SALT
- [ ] MALDON SALT
- [ ] EXTRA FINE SEA SALT
- [ ] FRENCH GRAY SEA SALT
- [ ] SMOKED SEA SALT
- [ ] SEL GRIS

BAKING CONDITIONS

HUMIDITY

TEMPERATURE

STARTER DESCRIPTION

FINISHED LOAF DESCRIPTION

CRUMB DESCRIPTORS

- [ ] EVEN, "TIGHT" HOLES
- [ ] EVEN, MEDIUM HOLES
- [ ] IRREGULAR, LARGE HOLES
- [ ] DELICATE STRUCTURE
- [ ] AVERAGE STRUCTURE
- [ ] STURDY STRUCTURE
- [ ] TRANSLUCENT
- [ ] DENSE
- [ ] COOL AND CREAMY
- [ ] DRY OR DUSTY
- [ ] OTHER _____

CRUST DESCRIPTORS

- [ ] TENDER, GOLDEN
- [ ] SOFT, COMPRESSIBLE
- [ ] HARD, CRUSTY
- [ ] CARAMELIZED
- [ ] NUTTY
- [ ] BUTTERY
- [ ] OILY
- [ ] TOOTHSOME
- [ ] CRISPY
- [ ] OTHER _____

DATE _____

INGREDIENTS

TYPES OF FLOUR

☐ ALL-PURPOSE
☐ UNBLEACHED ALL-PURPOSE
☐ BREAD FLOUR
☐ UNBLEACHED WHEAT
  ___ *Plus malted*
  ___ *Low ash*
  ___ *Malted All-purpose*
  ___ *High-gluten*
☐ WHOLE-WHEAT
  ___ *Fine*
  ___ *High-protein fine*
  ___ *Medium*
  ___ *High-protein medium*
  ___ *Coarse*
  ___ *High-protein coarse*
  ___ *Special medium/coarse*

☐ HARD WHITE WHOLE-WHEAT
☐ BROMATED HIGH-PROTEIN
☐ UNBLEACHED ENRICHED
☐ BLEACHED WHEAT
☐ ARTISAN BREAD
☐ IRISH-STYLE WHOLEMEAL
☐ HIGH-GLUTEN
☐ HIGH-EXTRACTION
  ___ *Type 70 malted*
  ___ *Stone ground type 80*
  ___ *Type 80*
  ___ *Old country type 85*
  ___ *Old country type 85 malted*
☐ OTHER _____

☐ SPECIALTY
  ___ *Barley*
  ___ *Coarse cornmeal*
  ___ *Fine cornmeal*
  ___ *Polenta*
  ___ *Flaxseed meal*
  ___ *Millet*
  ___ *Brown rice*
  ___ *White rice*
  ___ *Cream of rye*
  ___ *Pumpernickel rye*
  ___ *White rye*
  ___ *Whole dark rye*
  ___ *Spelt*
  ___ *Semolina*
  ___ *Whole durum*
  ___ *Whole-wheat durum*

TYPES OF SALT

☐ IODIZED TABLE SALT
☐ KOSHER MEDIUM-COARSE SALT
☐ PINK HIMALAYAN SALT
☐ VOLCANIC BLACK SALT
☐ MALDON SALT
☐ EXTRA FINE SEA SALT
☐ FRENCH GRAY SEA SALT
☐ SMOKED SEA SALT
☐ SEL GRIS

BAKING CONDITIONS

HUMIDITY

TEMPERATURE

STARTER DESCRIPTION

FINISHED LOAF DESCRIPTION

CRUMB DESCRIPTORS

☐ EVEN, "TIGHT" HOLES
☐ EVEN, MEDIUM HOLES
☐ IRREGULAR, LARGE HOLES
☐ DELICATE STRUCTURE
☐ AVERAGE STRUCTURE
☐ STURDY STRUCTURE
☐ TRANSLUCENT
☐ DENSE
☐ COOL AND CREAMY
☐ DRY OR DUSTY
☐ OTHER _____

CRUST DESCRIPTORS

☐ TENDER, GOLDEN
☐ SOFT, COMPRESSIBLE
☐ HARD, CRUSTY
☐ CARAMELIZED
☐ NUTTY
☐ BUTTERY
☐ OILY
☐ TOOTHSOME
☐ CRISPY
☐ OTHER _____

DATE _____

INGREDIENTS

TYPES OF FLOUR

- ☐ ALL-PURPOSE
- ☐ UNBLEACHED ALL-PURPOSE
- ☐ BREAD FLOUR
- ☐ UNBLEACHED WHEAT
  - ___ *Plus malted*
  - ___ *Low ash*
  - ___ *Malted All-purpose*
  - ___ *High-gluten*
- ☐ WHOLE-WHEAT
  - ___ *Fine*
  - ___ *High-protein fine*
  - ___ *Medium*
  - ___ *High-protein medium*
  - ___ *Coarse*
  - ___ *High-protein coarse*
  - ___ *Special medium/coarse*

- ☐ HARD WHITE WHOLE-WHEAT
- ☐ BROMATED HIGH-PROTEIN
- ☐ UNBLEACHED ENRICHED
- ☐ BLEACHED WHEAT
- ☐ ARTISAN BREAD
- ☐ IRISH-STYLE WHOLEMEAL
- ☐ HIGH-GLUTEN
- ☐ HIGH-EXTRACTION
  - ___ *Type 70 malted*
  - ___ *Stone ground type 80*
  - ___ *Type 80*
  - ___ *Old country type 85*
  - ___ *Old country type 85 malted*
- ☐ OTHER _____

- ☐ SPECIALTY
  - ___ *Barley*
  - ___ *Coarse cornmeal*
  - ___ *Fine cornmeal*
  - ___ *Polenta*
  - ___ *Flaxseed meal*
  - ___ *Millet*
  - ___ *Brown rice*
  - ___ *White rice*
  - ___ *Cream of rye*
  - ___ *Pumpernickel rye*
  - ___ *White rye*
  - ___ *Whole dark rye*
  - ___ *Spelt*
  - ___ *Semolina*
  - ___ *Whole durum*
  - ___ *Whole-wheat durum*

TYPES OF SALT

- ☐ IODIZED TABLE SALT
- ☐ KOSHER MEDIUM-COARSE SALT
- ☐ PINK HIMALAYAN SALT
- ☐ VOLCANIC BLACK SALT
- ☐ MALDON SALT
- ☐ EXTRA FINE SEA SALT
- ☐ FRENCH GRAY SEA SALT
- ☐ SMOKED SEA SALT
- ☐ SEL GRIS

BAKING CONDITIONS

HUMIDITY

TEMPERATURE

STARTER DESCRIPTION

FINISHED LOAF DESCRIPTION

CRUMB DESCRIPTORS

- ☐ EVEN, "TIGHT" HOLES
- ☐ EVEN, MEDIUM HOLES
- ☐ IRREGULAR, LARGE HOLES
- ☐ DELICATE STRUCTURE
- ☐ AVERAGE STRUCTURE
- ☐ STURDY STRUCTURE
- ☐ TRANSLUCENT
- ☐ DENSE
- ☐ COOL AND CREAMY
- ☐ DRY OR DUSTY
- ☐ OTHER _____

CRUST DESCRIPTORS

- ☐ TENDER, GOLDEN
- ☐ SOFT, COMPRESSIBLE
- ☐ HARD, CRUSTY
- ☐ CARAMELIZED
- ☐ NUTTY
- ☐ BUTTERY
- ☐ OILY
- ☐ TOOTHSOME
- ☐ CRISPY
- ☐ OTHER _____

DATE _____

INGREDIENTS

TYPES OF FLOUR

- ☐ ALL-PURPOSE
- ☐ UNBLEACHED ALL-PURPOSE
- ☐ BREAD FLOUR
- ☐ UNBLEACHED WHEAT
  - ___ *Plus malted*
  - ___ *Low ash*
  - ___ *Malted All-purpose*
  - ___ *High-gluten*
- ☐ WHOLE-WHEAT
  - ___ *Fine*
  - ___ *High-protein fine*
  - ___ *Medium*
  - ___ *High-protein medium*
  - ___ *Coarse*
  - ___ *High-protein coarse*
  - ___ *Special medium/coarse*

- ☐ HARD WHITE WHOLE-WHEAT
- ☐ BROMATED HIGH-PROTEIN
- ☐ UNBLEACHED ENRICHED
- ☐ BLEACHED WHEAT
- ☐ ARTISAN BREAD
- ☐ IRISH-STYLE WHOLEMEAL
- ☐ HIGH-GLUTEN
- ☐ HIGH-EXTRACTION
  - ___ *Type 70 malted*
  - ___ *Stone ground type 80*
  - ___ *Type 80*
  - ___ *Old country type 85*
  - ___ *Old country type 85 malted*
- ☐ OTHER _____

- ☐ SPECIALTY
  - ___ *Barley*
  - ___ *Coarse cornmeal*
  - ___ *Fine cornmeal*
  - ___ *Polenta*
  - ___ *Flaxseed meal*
  - ___ *Millet*
  - ___ *Brown rice*
  - ___ *White rice*
  - ___ *Cream of rye*
  - ___ *Pumpernickel rye*
  - ___ *White rye*
  - ___ *Whole dark rye*
  - ___ *Spelt*
  - ___ *Semolina*
  - ___ *Whole durum*
  - ___ *Whole-wheat durum*

TYPES OF SALT

- ☐ IODIZED TABLE SALT
- ☐ KOSHER MEDIUM-COARSE SALT
- ☐ PINK HIMALAYAN SALT
- ☐ VOLCANIC BLACK SALT
- ☐ MALDON SALT
- ☐ EXTRA FINE SEA SALT
- ☐ FRENCH GRAY SEA SALT
- ☐ SMOKED SEA SALT
- ☐ SEL GRIS

BAKING CONDITIONS

HUMIDITY

TEMPERATURE

STARTER DESCRIPTION

FINISHED LOAF DESCRIPTION

CRUMB DESCRIPTORS

- ☐ EVEN, "TIGHT" HOLES
- ☐ EVEN, MEDIUM HOLES
- ☐ IRREGULAR, LARGE HOLES
- ☐ DELICATE STRUCTURE
- ☐ AVERAGE STRUCTURE
- ☐ STURDY STRUCTURE
- ☐ TRANSLUCENT
- ☐ DENSE
- ☐ COOL AND CREAMY
- ☐ DRY OR DUSTY
- ☐ OTHER _____

CRUST DESCRIPTORS

- ☐ TENDER, GOLDEN
- ☐ SOFT, COMPRESSIBLE
- ☐ HARD, CRUSTY
- ☐ CARAMELIZED
- ☐ NUTTY
- ☐ BUTTERY
- ☐ OILY
- ☐ TOOTHSOME
- ☐ CRISPY
- ☐ OTHER _____

DATE _____

INGREDIENTS

TYPES OF FLOUR

- [ ] ALL-PURPOSE
- [ ] UNBLEACHED ALL-PURPOSE
- [ ] BREAD FLOUR
- [ ] UNBLEACHED WHEAT
  - ___ *Plus malted*
  - ___ *Low ash*
  - ___ *Malted All-purpose*
  - ___ *High-gluten*
- [ ] WHOLE-WHEAT
  - ___ *Fine*
  - ___ *High-protein fine*
  - ___ *Medium*
  - ___ *High-protein medium*
  - ___ *Coarse*
  - ___ *High-protein coarse*
  - ___ *Special medium/coarse*

- [ ] HARD WHITE WHOLE-WHEAT
- [ ] BROMATED HIGH-PROTEIN
- [ ] UNBLEACHED ENRICHED
- [ ] BLEACHED WHEAT
- [ ] ARTISAN BREAD
- [ ] IRISH-STYLE WHOLEMEAL
- [ ] HIGH-GLUTEN
- [ ] HIGH-EXTRACTION
  - ___ *Type 70 malted*
  - ___ *Stone ground type 80*
  - ___ *Type 80*
  - ___ *Old country type 85*
  - ___ *Old country type 85 malted*
- [ ] OTHER _____

- [ ] SPECIALTY
  - ___ *Barley*
  - ___ *Coarse cornmeal*
  - ___ *Fine cornmeal*
  - ___ *Polenta*
  - ___ *Flaxseed meal*
  - ___ *Millet*
  - ___ *Brown rice*
  - ___ *White rice*
  - ___ *Cream of rye*
  - ___ *Pumpernickel rye*
  - ___ *White rye*
  - ___ *Whole dark rye*
  - ___ *Spelt*
  - ___ *Semolina*
  - ___ *Whole durum*
  - ___ *Whole-wheat durum*

TYPES OF SALT

- [ ] IODIZED TABLE SALT
- [ ] KOSHER MEDIUM-COARSE SALT
- [ ] PINK HIMALAYAN SALT
- [ ] VOLCANIC BLACK SALT
- [ ] MALDON SALT
- [ ] EXTRA FINE SEA SALT
- [ ] FRENCH GRAY SEA SALT
- [ ] SMOKED SEA SALT
- [ ] SEL GRIS

BAKING CONDITIONS

HUMIDITY

TEMPERATURE

STARTER DESCRIPTION

FINISHED LOAF DESCRIPTION

CRUMB DESCRIPTORS

- [ ] EVEN, "TIGHT" HOLES
- [ ] EVEN, MEDIUM HOLES
- [ ] IRREGULAR, LARGE HOLES
- [ ] DELICATE STRUCTURE
- [ ] AVERAGE STRUCTURE
- [ ] STURDY STRUCTURE
- [ ] TRANSLUCENT
- [ ] DENSE
- [ ] COOL AND CREAMY
- [ ] DRY OR DUSTY
- [ ] OTHER _____

CRUST DESCRIPTORS

- [ ] TENDER, GOLDEN
- [ ] SOFT, COMPRESSIBLE
- [ ] HARD, CRUSTY
- [ ] CARAMELIZED
- [ ] NUTTY
- [ ] BUTTERY
- [ ] OILY
- [ ] TOOTHSOME
- [ ] CRISPY
- [ ] OTHER _____

DATE _____

NOTES

INGREDIENTS

TYPES OF FLOUR

- ☐ ALL-PURPOSE
- ☐ UNBLEACHED ALL-PURPOSE
- ☐ BREAD FLOUR
- ☐ UNBLEACHED WHEAT
  - ___ *Plus malted*
  - ___ *Low ash*
  - ___ *Malted All-purpose*
  - ___ *High-gluten*
- ☐ WHOLE-WHEAT
  - ___ *Fine*
  - ___ *High-protein fine*
  - ___ *Medium*
  - ___ *High-protein medium*
  - ___ *Coarse*
  - ___ *High-protein coarse*
  - ___ *Special medium/coarse*

- ☐ HARD WHITE WHOLE-WHEAT
- ☐ BROMATED HIGH-PROTEIN
- ☐ UNBLEACHED ENRICHED
- ☐ BLEACHED WHEAT
- ☐ ARTISAN BREAD
- ☐ IRISH-STYLE WHOLEMEAL
- ☐ HIGH-GLUTEN
- ☐ HIGH-EXTRACTION
  - ___ *Type 70 malted*
  - ___ *Stone ground type 80*
  - ___ *Type 80*
  - ___ *Old country type 85*
  - ___ *Old country type 85 malted*
- ☐ OTHER _____

- ☐ SPECIALTY
  - ___ *Barley*
  - ___ *Coarse cornmeal*
  - ___ *Fine cornmeal*
  - ___ *Polenta*
  - ___ *Flaxseed meal*
  - ___ *Millet*
  - ___ *Brown rice*
  - ___ *White rice*
  - ___ *Cream of rye*
  - ___ *Pumpernickel rye*
  - ___ *White rye*
  - ___ *Whole dark rye*
  - ___ *Spelt*
  - ___ *Semolina*
  - ___ *Whole durum*
  - ___ *Whole-wheat durum*

TYPES OF SALT

- ☐ IODIZED TABLE SALT
- ☐ KOSHER MEDIUM-COARSE SALT
- ☐ PINK HIMALAYAN SALT
- ☐ VOLCANIC BLACK SALT
- ☐ MALDON SALT
- ☐ EXTRA FINE SEA SALT
- ☐ FRENCH GRAY SEA SALT
- ☐ SMOKED SEA SALT
- ☐ SEL GRIS

BAKING CONDITIONS

HUMIDITY

TEMPERATURE

STARTER DESCRIPTION

FINISHED LOAF DESCRIPTION

CRUMB DESCRIPTORS

- ☐ EVEN, "TIGHT" HOLES
- ☐ EVEN, MEDIUM HOLES
- ☐ IRREGULAR, LARGE HOLES
- ☐ DELICATE STRUCTURE
- ☐ AVERAGE STRUCTURE
- ☐ STURDY STRUCTURE
- ☐ TRANSLUCENT
- ☐ DENSE
- ☐ COOL AND CREAMY
- ☐ DRY OR DUSTY
- ☐ OTHER _____

CRUST DESCRIPTORS

- ☐ TENDER, GOLDEN
- ☐ SOFT, COMPRESSIBLE
- ☐ HARD, CRUSTY
- ☐ CARAMELIZED
- ☐ NUTTY
- ☐ BUTTERY
- ☐ OILY
- ☐ TOOTHSOME
- ☐ CRISPY
- ☐ OTHER _____

DATE _____

INGREDIENTS

TYPES OF FLOUR

- ☐ ALL-PURPOSE
- ☐ UNBLEACHED ALL-PURPOSE
- ☐ BREAD FLOUR
- ☐ UNBLEACHED WHEAT
  - ___ *Plus malted*
  - ___ *Low ash*
  - ___ *Malted All-purpose*
  - ___ *High-gluten*
- ☐ WHOLE-WHEAT
  - ___ *Fine*
  - ___ *High-protein fine*
  - ___ *Medium*
  - ___ *High-protein medium*
  - ___ *Coarse*
  - ___ *High-protein coarse*
  - ___ *Special medium/coarse*

- ☐ HARD WHITE WHOLE-WHEAT
- ☐ BROMATED HIGH-PROTEIN
- ☐ UNBLEACHED ENRICHED
- ☐ BLEACHED WHEAT
- ☐ ARTISAN BREAD
- ☐ IRISH-STYLE WHOLEMEAL
- ☐ HIGH-GLUTEN
- ☐ HIGH-EXTRACTION
  - ___ *Type 70 malted*
  - ___ *Stone ground type 80*
  - ___ *Type 80*
  - ___ *Old country type 85*
  - ___ *Old country type 85 malted*
- ☐ OTHER _____

- ☐ SPECIALTY
  - ___ *Barley*
  - ___ *Coarse cornmeal*
  - ___ *Fine cornmeal*
  - ___ *Polenta*
  - ___ *Flaxseed meal*
  - ___ *Millet*
  - ___ *Brown rice*
  - ___ *White rice*
  - ___ *Cream of rye*
  - ___ *Pumpernickel rye*
  - ___ *White rye*
  - ___ *Whole dark rye*
  - ___ *Spelt*
  - ___ *Semolina*
  - ___ *Whole durum*
  - ___ *Whole-wheat durum*

TYPES OF SALT

- ☐ IODIZED TABLE SALT
- ☐ KOSHER MEDIUM-COARSE SALT
- ☐ PINK HIMALAYAN SALT
- ☐ VOLCANIC BLACK SALT
- ☐ MALDON SALT
- ☐ EXTRA FINE SEA SALT
- ☐ FRENCH GRAY SEA SALT
- ☐ SMOKED SEA SALT
- ☐ SEL GRIS

BAKING CONDITIONS

HUMIDITY

TEMPERATURE

STARTER DESCRIPTION

FINISHED LOAF DESCRIPTION

CRUMB DESCRIPTORS

- ☐ EVEN, "TIGHT" HOLES
- ☐ EVEN, MEDIUM HOLES
- ☐ IRREGULAR, LARGE HOLES
- ☐ DELICATE STRUCTURE
- ☐ AVERAGE STRUCTURE
- ☐ STURDY STRUCTURE
- ☐ TRANSLUCENT
- ☐ DENSE
- ☐ COOL AND CREAMY
- ☐ DRY OR DUSTY
- ☐ OTHER _____

CRUST DESCRIPTORS

- ☐ TENDER, GOLDEN
- ☐ SOFT, COMPRESSIBLE
- ☐ HARD, CRUSTY
- ☐ CARAMELIZED
- ☐ NUTTY
- ☐ BUTTERY
- ☐ OILY
- ☐ TOOTHSOME
- ☐ CRISPY
- ☐ OTHER _____

DATE _____

NOTES

INGREDIENTS

TYPES OF FLOUR

- ☐ ALL-PURPOSE
- ☐ UNBLEACHED ALL-PURPOSE
- ☐ BREAD FLOUR
- ☐ UNBLEACHED WHEAT
  - ___ *Plus malted*
  - ___ *Low ash*
  - ___ *Malted All-purpose*
  - ___ *High-gluten*
- ☐ WHOLE-WHEAT
  - ___ *Fine*
  - ___ *High-protein fine*
  - ___ *Medium*
  - ___ *High-protein medium*
  - ___ *Coarse*
  - ___ *High-protein coarse*
  - ___ *Special medium/coarse*

- ☐ HARD WHITE WHOLE-WHEAT
- ☐ BROMATED HIGH-PROTEIN
- ☐ UNBLEACHED ENRICHED
- ☐ BLEACHED WHEAT
- ☐ ARTISAN BREAD
- ☐ IRISH-STYLE WHOLEMEAL
- ☐ HIGH-GLUTEN
- ☐ HIGH-EXTRACTION
  - ___ *Type 70 malted*
  - ___ *Stone ground type 80*
  - ___ *Type 80*
  - ___ *Old country type 85*
  - ___ *Old country type 85 malted*
- ☐ OTHER _____

- ☐ SPECIALTY
  - ___ *Barley*
  - ___ *Coarse cornmeal*
  - ___ *Fine cornmeal*
  - ___ *Polenta*
  - ___ *Flaxseed meal*
  - ___ *Millet*
  - ___ *Brown rice*
  - ___ *White rice*
  - ___ *Cream of rye*
  - ___ *Pumpernickel rye*
  - ___ *White rye*
  - ___ *Whole dark rye*
  - ___ *Spelt*
  - ___ *Semolina*
  - ___ *Whole durum*
  - ___ *Whole-wheat durum*

TYPES OF SALT

- ☐ IODIZED TABLE SALT
- ☐ KOSHER MEDIUM-COARSE SALT
- ☐ PINK HIMALAYAN SALT
- ☐ VOLCANIC BLACK SALT
- ☐ MALDON SALT
- ☐ EXTRA FINE SEA SALT
- ☐ FRENCH GRAY SEA SALT
- ☐ SMOKED SEA SALT
- ☐ SEL GRIS

BAKING CONDITIONS

HUMIDITY

TEMPERATURE

STARTER DESCRIPTION

FINISHED LOAF DESCRIPTION

CRUMB DESCRIPTORS

- ☐ EVEN, "TIGHT" HOLES
- ☐ EVEN, MEDIUM HOLES
- ☐ IRREGULAR, LARGE HOLES
- ☐ DELICATE STRUCTURE
- ☐ AVERAGE STRUCTURE
- ☐ STURDY STRUCTURE
- ☐ TRANSLUCENT
- ☐ DENSE
- ☐ COOL AND CREAMY
- ☐ DRY OR DUSTY
- ☐ OTHER _____

CRUST DESCRIPTORS

- ☐ TENDER, GOLDEN
- ☐ SOFT, COMPRESSIBLE
- ☐ HARD, CRUSTY
- ☐ CARAMELIZED
- ☐ NUTTY
- ☐ BUTTERY
- ☐ OILY
- ☐ TOOTHSOME
- ☐ CRISPY
- ☐ OTHER _____

DATE _____

NOTES

INGREDIENTS

TYPES OF FLOUR

- ☐ ALL-PURPOSE
- ☐ UNBLEACHED ALL-PURPOSE
- ☐ BREAD FLOUR
- ☐ UNBLEACHED WHEAT
  - ___ *Plus malted*
  - ___ *Low ash*
  - ___ *Malted All-purpose*
  - ___ *High-gluten*
- ☐ WHOLE-WHEAT
  - ___ *Fine*
  - ___ *High-protein fine*
  - ___ *Medium*
  - ___ *High-protein medium*
  - ___ *Coarse*
  - ___ *High-protein coarse*
  - ___ *Special medium/coarse*

- ☐ HARD WHITE WHOLE-WHEAT
- ☐ BROMATED HIGH-PROTEIN
- ☐ UNBLEACHED ENRICHED
- ☐ BLEACHED WHEAT
- ☐ ARTISAN BREAD
- ☐ IRISH-STYLE WHOLEMEAL
- ☐ HIGH-GLUTEN
- ☐ HIGH-EXTRACTION
  - ___ *Type 70 malted*
  - ___ *Stone ground type 80*
  - ___ *Type 80*
  - ___ *Old country type 85*
  - ___ *Old country type 85 malted*
- ☐ OTHER _____

- ☐ SPECIALTY
  - ___ *Barley*
  - ___ *Coarse cornmeal*
  - ___ *Fine cornmeal*
  - ___ *Polenta*
  - ___ *Flaxseed meal*
  - ___ *Millet*
  - ___ *Brown rice*
  - ___ *White rice*
  - ___ *Cream of rye*
  - ___ *Pumpernickel rye*
  - ___ *White rye*
  - ___ *Whole dark rye*
  - ___ *Spelt*
  - ___ *Semolina*
  - ___ *Whole durum*
  - ___ *Whole-wheat durum*

TYPES OF SALT

- ☐ IODIZED TABLE SALT
- ☐ KOSHER MEDIUM-COARSE SALT
- ☐ PINK HIMALAYAN SALT
- ☐ VOLCANIC BLACK SALT
- ☐ MALDON SALT
- ☐ EXTRA FINE SEA SALT
- ☐ FRENCH GRAY SEA SALT
- ☐ SMOKED SEA SALT
- ☐ SEL GRIS

BAKING CONDITIONS

HUMIDITY

TEMPERATURE

STARTER DESCRIPTION

FINISHED LOAF DESCRIPTION

CRUMB DESCRIPTORS

- ☐ EVEN, "TIGHT" HOLES
- ☐ EVEN, MEDIUM HOLES
- ☐ IRREGULAR, LARGE HOLES
- ☐ DELICATE STRUCTURE
- ☐ AVERAGE STRUCTURE
- ☐ STURDY STRUCTURE
- ☐ TRANSLUCENT
- ☐ DENSE
- ☐ COOL AND CREAMY
- ☐ DRY OR DUSTY
- ☐ OTHER _____

CRUST DESCRIPTORS

- ☐ TENDER, GOLDEN
- ☐ SOFT, COMPRESSIBLE
- ☐ HARD, CRUSTY
- ☐ CARAMELIZED
- ☐ NUTTY
- ☐ BUTTERY
- ☐ OILY
- ☐ TOOTHSOME
- ☐ CRISPY
- ☐ OTHER _____

DATE _____

INGREDIENTS

TYPES OF FLOUR

- ☐ ALL-PURPOSE
- ☐ UNBLEACHED ALL-PURPOSE
- ☐ BREAD FLOUR
- ☐ UNBLEACHED WHEAT
  - ___ *Plus malted*
  - ___ *Low ash*
  - ___ *Malted All-purpose*
  - ___ *High-gluten*
- ☐ WHOLE-WHEAT
  - ___ *Fine*
  - ___ *High-protein fine*
  - ___ *Medium*
  - ___ *High-protein medium*
  - ___ *Coarse*
  - ___ *High-protein coarse*
  - ___ *Special medium/coarse*

- ☐ HARD WHITE WHOLE-WHEAT
- ☐ BROMATED HIGH-PROTEIN
- ☐ UNBLEACHED ENRICHED
- ☐ BLEACHED WHEAT
- ☐ ARTISAN BREAD
- ☐ IRISH-STYLE WHOLEMEAL
- ☐ HIGH-GLUTEN
- ☐ HIGH-EXTRACTION
  - ___ *Type 70 malted*
  - ___ *Stone ground type 80*
  - ___ *Type 80*
  - ___ *Old country type 85*
  - ___ *Old country type 85 malted*
- ☐ OTHER _____

- ☐ SPECIALTY
  - ___ *Barley*
  - ___ *Coarse cornmeal*
  - ___ *Fine cornmeal*
  - ___ *Polenta*
  - ___ *Flaxseed meal*
  - ___ *Millet*
  - ___ *Brown rice*
  - ___ *White rice*
  - ___ *Cream of rye*
  - ___ *Pumpernickel rye*
  - ___ *White rye*
  - ___ *Whole dark rye*
  - ___ *Spelt*
  - ___ *Semolina*
  - ___ *Whole durum*
  - ___ *Whole-wheat durum*

TYPES OF SALT

- ☐ IODIZED TABLE SALT
- ☐ KOSHER MEDIUM-COARSE SALT
- ☐ PINK HIMALAYAN SALT
- ☐ VOLCANIC BLACK SALT
- ☐ MALDON SALT
- ☐ EXTRA FINE SEA SALT
- ☐ FRENCH GRAY SEA SALT
- ☐ SMOKED SEA SALT
- ☐ SEL GRIS

BAKING CONDITIONS

HUMIDITY

TEMPERATURE

STARTER DESCRIPTION

FINISHED LOAF DESCRIPTION

CRUMB DESCRIPTORS

- ☐ EVEN, "TIGHT" HOLES
- ☐ EVEN, MEDIUM HOLES
- ☐ IRREGULAR, LARGE HOLES
- ☐ DELICATE STRUCTURE
- ☐ AVERAGE STRUCTURE
- ☐ STURDY STRUCTURE
- ☐ TRANSLUCENT
- ☐ DENSE
- ☐ COOL AND CREAMY
- ☐ DRY OR DUSTY
- ☐ OTHER _____

CRUST DESCRIPTORS

- ☐ TENDER, GOLDEN
- ☐ SOFT, COMPRESSIBLE
- ☐ HARD, CRUSTY
- ☐ CARAMELIZED
- ☐ NUTTY
- ☐ BUTTERY
- ☐ OILY
- ☐ TOOTHSOME
- ☐ CRISPY
- ☐ OTHER _____

DATE _____

INGREDIENTS

TYPES OF FLOUR

- ☐ ALL-PURPOSE
- ☐ UNBLEACHED ALL-PURPOSE
- ☐ BREAD FLOUR
- ☐ UNBLEACHED WHEAT
  - ___ *Plus malted*
  - ___ *Low ash*
  - ___ *Malted All-purpose*
  - ___ *High-gluten*
- ☐ WHOLE-WHEAT
  - ___ *Fine*
  - ___ *High-protein fine*
  - ___ *Medium*
  - ___ *High-protein medium*
  - ___ *Coarse*
  - ___ *High-protein coarse*
  - ___ *Special medium/coarse*

- ☐ HARD WHITE WHOLE-WHEAT
- ☐ BROMATED HIGH-PROTEIN
- ☐ UNBLEACHED ENRICHED
- ☐ BLEACHED WHEAT
- ☐ ARTISAN BREAD
- ☐ IRISH-STYLE WHOLEMEAL
- ☐ HIGH-GLUTEN
- ☐ HIGH-EXTRACTION
  - ___ *Type 70 malted*
  - ___ *Stone ground type 80*
  - ___ *Type 80*
  - ___ *Old country type 85*
  - ___ *Old country type 85 malted*
- ☐ OTHER _____

- ☐ SPECIALTY
  - ___ *Barley*
  - ___ *Coarse cornmeal*
  - ___ *Fine cornmeal*
  - ___ *Polenta*
  - ___ *Flaxseed meal*
  - ___ *Millet*
  - ___ *Brown rice*
  - ___ *White rice*
  - ___ *Cream of rye*
  - ___ *Pumpernickel rye*
  - ___ *White rye*
  - ___ *Whole dark rye*
  - ___ *Spelt*
  - ___ *Semolina*
  - ___ *Whole durum*
  - ___ *Whole-wheat durum*

TYPES OF SALT

- ☐ IODIZED TABLE SALT
- ☐ KOSHER MEDIUM-COARSE SALT
- ☐ PINK HIMALAYAN SALT
- ☐ VOLCANIC BLACK SALT
- ☐ MALDON SALT
- ☐ EXTRA FINE SEA SALT
- ☐ FRENCH GRAY SEA SALT
- ☐ SMOKED SEA SALT
- ☐ SEL GRIS

BAKING CONDITIONS

HUMIDITY

TEMPERATURE

STARTER DESCRIPTION

FINISHED LOAF DESCRIPTION

CRUMB DESCRIPTORS

- ☐ EVEN, "TIGHT" HOLES
- ☐ EVEN, MEDIUM HOLES
- ☐ IRREGULAR, LARGE HOLES
- ☐ DELICATE STRUCTURE
- ☐ AVERAGE STRUCTURE
- ☐ STURDY STRUCTURE
- ☐ TRANSLUCENT
- ☐ DENSE
- ☐ COOL AND CREAMY
- ☐ DRY OR DUSTY
- ☐ OTHER _____

CRUST DESCRIPTORS

- ☐ TENDER, GOLDEN
- ☐ SOFT, COMPRESSIBLE
- ☐ HARD, CRUSTY
- ☐ CARAMELIZED
- ☐ NUTTY
- ☐ BUTTERY
- ☐ OILY
- ☐ TOOTHSOME
- ☐ CRISPY
- ☐ OTHER _____

DATE _____

NOTES

INGREDIENTS

TYPES OF FLOUR

☐ ALL-PURPOSE
☐ UNBLEACHED ALL-PURPOSE
☐ BREAD FLOUR
☐ UNBLEACHED WHEAT
    ___ *Plus malted*
    ___ *Low ash*
    ___ *Malted All-purpose*
    ___ *High-gluten*
☐ WHOLE-WHEAT
    ___ *Fine*
    ___ *High-protein fine*
    ___ *Medium*
    ___ *High-protein medium*
    ___ *Coarse*
    ___ *High-protein coarse*
    ___ *Special medium/coarse*

☐ HARD WHITE WHOLE-WHEAT
☐ BROMATED HIGH-PROTEIN
☐ UNBLEACHED ENRICHED
☐ BLEACHED WHEAT
☐ ARTISAN BREAD
☐ IRISH-STYLE WHOLEMEAL
☐ HIGH-GLUTEN
☐ HIGH-EXTRACTION
    ___ *Type 70 malted*
    ___ *Stone ground type 80*
    ___ *Type 80*
    ___ *Old country type 85*
    ___ *Old country type 85 malted*
☐ OTHER _____

☐ SPECIALTY
    ___ *Barley*
    ___ *Coarse cornmeal*
    ___ *Fine cornmeal*
    ___ *Polenta*
    ___ *Flaxseed meal*
    ___ *Millet*
    ___ *Brown rice*
    ___ *White rice*
    ___ *Cream of rye*
    ___ *Pumpernickel rye*
    ___ *White rye*
    ___ *Whole dark rye*
    ___ *Spelt*
    ___ *Semolina*
    ___ *Whole durum*
    ___ *Whole-wheat durum*

TYPES OF SALT

☐ IODIZED TABLE SALT
☐ KOSHER MEDIUM-COARSE SALT
☐ PINK HIMALAYAN SALT
☐ VOLCANIC BLACK SALT
☐ MALDON SALT
☐ EXTRA FINE SEA SALT
☐ FRENCH GRAY SEA SALT
☐ SMOKED SEA SALT
☐ SEL GRIS

BAKING CONDITIONS

HUMIDITY

TEMPERATURE

STARTER DESCRIPTION

FINISHED LOAF DESCRIPTION

CRUMB DESCRIPTORS

☐ EVEN, "TIGHT" HOLES
☐ EVEN, MEDIUM HOLES
☐ IRREGULAR, LARGE HOLES
☐ DELICATE STRUCTURE
☐ AVERAGE STRUCTURE
☐ STURDY STRUCTURE
☐ TRANSLUCENT
☐ DENSE
☐ COOL AND CREAMY
☐ DRY OR DUSTY
☐ OTHER _____

CRUST DESCRIPTORS

☐ TENDER, GOLDEN
☐ SOFT, COMPRESSIBLE
☐ HARD, CRUSTY
☐ CARAMELIZED
☐ NUTTY
☐ BUTTERY
☐ OILY
☐ TOOTHSOME
☐ CRISPY
☐ OTHER _____

DATE _____

INGREDIENTS

TYPES OF FLOUR

- ☐ ALL-PURPOSE
- ☐ UNBLEACHED ALL-PURPOSE
- ☐ BREAD FLOUR
- ☐ UNBLEACHED WHEAT
  - ___ *Plus malted*
  - ___ *Low ash*
  - ___ *Malted All-purpose*
  - ___ *High-gluten*
- ☐ WHOLE-WHEAT
  - ___ *Fine*
  - ___ *High-protein fine*
  - ___ *Medium*
  - ___ *High-protein medium*
  - ___ *Coarse*
  - ___ *High-protein coarse*
  - ___ *Special medium/coarse*

- ☐ HARD WHITE WHOLE-WHEAT
- ☐ BROMATED HIGH-PROTEIN
- ☐ UNBLEACHED ENRICHED
- ☐ BLEACHED WHEAT
- ☐ ARTISAN BREAD
- ☐ IRISH-STYLE WHOLEMEAL
- ☐ HIGH-GLUTEN
- ☐ HIGH-EXTRACTION
  - ___ *Type 70 malted*
  - ___ *Stone ground type 80*
  - ___ *Type 80*
  - ___ *Old country type 85*
  - ___ *Old country type 85 malted*
- ☐ OTHER _____

- ☐ SPECIALTY
  - ___ *Barley*
  - ___ *Coarse cornmeal*
  - ___ *Fine cornmeal*
  - ___ *Polenta*
  - ___ *Flaxseed meal*
  - ___ *Millet*
  - ___ *Brown rice*
  - ___ *White rice*
  - ___ *Cream of rye*
  - ___ *Pumpernickel rye*
  - ___ *White rye*
  - ___ *Whole dark rye*
  - ___ *Spelt*
  - ___ *Semolina*
  - ___ *Whole durum*
  - ___ *Whole-wheat durum*

TYPES OF SALT

- ☐ IODIZED TABLE SALT
- ☐ KOSHER MEDIUM-COARSE SALT
- ☐ PINK HIMALAYAN SALT
- ☐ VOLCANIC BLACK SALT
- ☐ MALDON SALT
- ☐ EXTRA FINE SEA SALT
- ☐ FRENCH GRAY SEA SALT
- ☐ SMOKED SEA SALT
- ☐ SEL GRIS

BAKING CONDITIONS

HUMIDITY

TEMPERATURE

STARTER DESCRIPTION

FINISHED LOAF DESCRIPTION

CRUMB DESCRIPTORS

- ☐ EVEN, "TIGHT" HOLES
- ☐ EVEN, MEDIUM HOLES
- ☐ IRREGULAR, LARGE HOLES
- ☐ DELICATE STRUCTURE
- ☐ AVERAGE STRUCTURE
- ☐ STURDY STRUCTURE
- ☐ TRANSLUCENT
- ☐ DENSE
- ☐ COOL AND CREAMY
- ☐ DRY OR DUSTY
- ☐ OTHER _____

CRUST DESCRIPTORS

- ☐ TENDER, GOLDEN
- ☐ SOFT, COMPRESSIBLE
- ☐ HARD, CRUSTY
- ☐ CARAMELIZED
- ☐ NUTTY
- ☐ BUTTERY
- ☐ OILY
- ☐ TOOTHSOME
- ☐ CRISPY
- ☐ OTHER _____

DATE _____

NOTES

INGREDIENTS

TYPES OF FLOUR

☐ ALL-PURPOSE
☐ UNBLEACHED ALL-PURPOSE
☐ BREAD FLOUR
☐ UNBLEACHED WHEAT
   ___ *Plus malted*
   ___ *Low ash*
   ___ *Malted All-purpose*
   ___ *High-gluten*
☐ WHOLE-WHEAT
   ___ *Fine*
   ___ *High-protein fine*
   ___ *Medium*
   ___ *High-protein medium*
   ___ *Coarse*
   ___ *High-protein coarse*
   ___ *Special medium/coarse*

☐ HARD WHITE WHOLE-WHEAT
☐ BROMATED HIGH-PROTEIN
☐ UNBLEACHED ENRICHED
☐ BLEACHED WHEAT
☐ ARTISAN BREAD
☐ IRISH-STYLE WHOLEMEAL
☐ HIGH-GLUTEN
☐ HIGH-EXTRACTION
   ___ *Type 70 malted*
   ___ *Stone ground type 80*
   ___ *Type 80*
   ___ *Old country type 85*
   ___ *Old country type 85 malted*
☐ OTHER _____

☐ SPECIALTY
   ___ *Barley*
   ___ *Coarse cornmeal*
   ___ *Fine cornmeal*
   ___ *Polenta*
   ___ *Flaxseed meal*
   ___ *Millet*
   ___ *Brown rice*
   ___ *White rice*
   ___ *Cream of rye*
   ___ *Pumpernickel rye*
   ___ *White rye*
   ___ *Whole dark rye*
   ___ *Spelt*
   ___ *Semolina*
   ___ *Whole durum*
   ___ *Whole-wheat durum*

TYPES OF SALT

☐ IODIZED TABLE SALT
☐ KOSHER MEDIUM-COARSE SALT
☐ PINK HIMALAYAN SALT
☐ VOLCANIC BLACK SALT
☐ MALDON SALT
☐ EXTRA FINE SEA SALT
☐ FRENCH GRAY SEA SALT
☐ SMOKED SEA SALT
☐ SEL GRIS

BAKING CONDITIONS

HUMIDITY

TEMPERATURE

STARTER DESCRIPTION

FINISHED LOAF DESCRIPTION

CRUMB DESCRIPTORS

☐ EVEN, "TIGHT" HOLES
☐ EVEN, MEDIUM HOLES
☐ IRREGULAR, LARGE HOLES
☐ DELICATE STRUCTURE
☐ AVERAGE STRUCTURE
☐ STURDY STRUCTURE
☐ TRANSLUCENT
☐ DENSE
☐ COOL AND CREAMY
☐ DRY OR DUSTY
☐ OTHER _____

CRUST DESCRIPTORS

☐ TENDER, GOLDEN
☐ SOFT, COMPRESSIBLE
☐ HARD, CRUSTY
☐ CARAMELIZED
☐ NUTTY
☐ BUTTERY
☐ OILY
☐ TOOTHSOME
☐ CRISPY
☐ OTHER _____

DATE _____

INGREDIENTS

TYPES OF FLOUR

- ☐ ALL-PURPOSE
- ☐ UNBLEACHED ALL-PURPOSE
- ☐ BREAD FLOUR
- ☐ UNBLEACHED WHEAT
  - ___ *Plus malted*
  - ___ *Low ash*
  - ___ *Malted All-purpose*
  - ___ *High-gluten*
- ☐ WHOLE-WHEAT
  - ___ *Fine*
  - ___ *High-protein fine*
  - ___ *Medium*
  - ___ *High-protein medium*
  - ___ *Coarse*
  - ___ *High-protein coarse*
  - ___ *Special medium/coarse*

- ☐ HARD WHITE WHOLE-WHEAT
- ☐ BROMATED HIGH-PROTEIN
- ☐ UNBLEACHED ENRICHED
- ☐ BLEACHED WHEAT
- ☐ ARTISAN BREAD
- ☐ IRISH-STYLE WHOLEMEAL
- ☐ HIGH-GLUTEN
- ☐ HIGH-EXTRACTION
  - ___ *Type 70 malted*
  - ___ *Stone ground type 80*
  - ___ *Type 80*
  - ___ *Old country type 85*
  - ___ *Old country type 85 malted*
- ☐ OTHER _____

- ☐ SPECIALTY
  - ___ *Barley*
  - ___ *Coarse cornmeal*
  - ___ *Fine cornmeal*
  - ___ *Polenta*
  - ___ *Flaxseed meal*
  - ___ *Millet*
  - ___ *Brown rice*
  - ___ *White rice*
  - ___ *Cream of rye*
  - ___ *Pumpernickel rye*
  - ___ *White rye*
  - ___ *Whole dark rye*
  - ___ *Spelt*
  - ___ *Semolina*
  - ___ *Whole durum*
  - ___ *Whole-wheat durum*

TYPES OF SALT

- ☐ IODIZED TABLE SALT
- ☐ KOSHER MEDIUM-COARSE SALT
- ☐ PINK HIMALAYAN SALT
- ☐ VOLCANIC BLACK SALT
- ☐ MALDON SALT
- ☐ EXTRA FINE SEA SALT
- ☐ FRENCH GRAY SEA SALT
- ☐ SMOKED SEA SALT
- ☐ SEL GRIS

BAKING CONDITIONS

HUMIDITY

TEMPERATURE

STARTER DESCRIPTION

FINISHED LOAF DESCRIPTION

CRUMB DESCRIPTORS

- ☐ EVEN, "TIGHT" HOLES
- ☐ EVEN, MEDIUM HOLES
- ☐ IRREGULAR, LARGE HOLES
- ☐ DELICATE STRUCTURE
- ☐ AVERAGE STRUCTURE
- ☐ STURDY STRUCTURE
- ☐ TRANSLUCENT
- ☐ DENSE
- ☐ COOL AND CREAMY
- ☐ DRY OR DUSTY
- ☐ OTHER _____

CRUST DESCRIPTORS

- ☐ TENDER, GOLDEN
- ☐ SOFT, COMPRESSIBLE
- ☐ HARD, CRUSTY
- ☐ CARAMELIZED
- ☐ NUTTY
- ☐ BUTTERY
- ☐ OILY
- ☐ TOOTHSOME
- ☐ CRISPY
- ☐ OTHER _____

DATE _____

NOTES

INGREDIENTS

TYPES OF FLOUR

- ☐ ALL-PURPOSE
- ☐ UNBLEACHED ALL-PURPOSE
- ☐ BREAD FLOUR
- ☐ UNBLEACHED WHEAT
  - ___ *Plus malted*
  - ___ *Low ash*
  - ___ *Malted All-purpose*
  - ___ *High-gluten*
- ☐ WHOLE-WHEAT
  - ___ *Fine*
  - ___ *High-protein fine*
  - ___ *Medium*
  - ___ *High-protein medium*
  - ___ *Coarse*
  - ___ *High-protein coarse*
  - ___ *Special medium/coarse*

- ☐ HARD WHITE WHOLE-WHEAT
- ☐ BROMATED HIGH-PROTEIN
- ☐ UNBLEACHED ENRICHED
- ☐ BLEACHED WHEAT
- ☐ ARTISAN BREAD
- ☐ IRISH-STYLE WHOLEMEAL
- ☐ HIGH-GLUTEN
- ☐ HIGH-EXTRACTION
  - ___ *Type 70 malted*
  - ___ *Stone ground type 80*
  - ___ *Type 80*
  - ___ *Old country type 85*
  - ___ *Old country type 85 malted*
- ☐ OTHER _____

- ☐ SPECIALTY
  - ___ *Barley*
  - ___ *Coarse cornmeal*
  - ___ *Fine cornmeal*
  - ___ *Polenta*
  - ___ *Flaxseed meal*
  - ___ *Millet*
  - ___ *Brown rice*
  - ___ *White rice*
  - ___ *Cream of rye*
  - ___ *Pumpernickel rye*
  - ___ *White rye*
  - ___ *Whole dark rye*
  - ___ *Spelt*
  - ___ *Semolina*
  - ___ *Whole durum*
  - ___ *Whole-wheat durum*

TYPES OF SALT

- ☐ IODIZED TABLE SALT
- ☐ KOSHER MEDIUM-COARSE SALT
- ☐ PINK HIMALAYAN SALT
- ☐ VOLCANIC BLACK SALT
- ☐ MALDON SALT
- ☐ EXTRA FINE SEA SALT
- ☐ FRENCH GRAY SEA SALT
- ☐ SMOKED SEA SALT
- ☐ SEL GRIS

BAKING CONDITIONS

HUMIDITY

TEMPERATURE

STARTER DESCRIPTION

FINISHED LOAF DESCRIPTION

CRUMB DESCRIPTORS

- ☐ EVEN, "TIGHT" HOLES
- ☐ EVEN, MEDIUM HOLES
- ☐ IRREGULAR, LARGE HOLES
- ☐ DELICATE STRUCTURE
- ☐ AVERAGE STRUCTURE
- ☐ STURDY STRUCTURE
- ☐ TRANSLUCENT
- ☐ DENSE
- ☐ COOL AND CREAMY
- ☐ DRY OR DUSTY
- ☐ OTHER _____

CRUST DESCRIPTORS

- ☐ TENDER, GOLDEN
- ☐ SOFT, COMPRESSIBLE
- ☐ HARD, CRUSTY
- ☐ CARAMELIZED
- ☐ NUTTY
- ☐ BUTTERY
- ☐ OILY
- ☐ TOOTHSOME
- ☐ CRISPY
- ☐ OTHER _____

DATE _____

NOTES

INGREDIENTS

TYPES OF FLOUR

- ☐ ALL-PURPOSE
- ☐ UNBLEACHED ALL-PURPOSE
- ☐ BREAD FLOUR
- ☐ UNBLEACHED WHEAT
  - ___ *Plus malted*
  - ___ *Low ash*
  - ___ *Malted All-purpose*
  - ___ *High-gluten*
- ☐ WHOLE-WHEAT
  - ___ *Fine*
  - ___ *High-protein fine*
  - ___ *Medium*
  - ___ *High-protein medium*
  - ___ *Coarse*
  - ___ *High-protein coarse*
  - ___ *Special medium/coarse*

- ☐ HARD WHITE WHOLE-WHEAT
- ☐ BROMATED HIGH-PROTEIN
- ☐ UNBLEACHED ENRICHED
- ☐ BLEACHED WHEAT
- ☐ ARTISAN BREAD
- ☐ IRISH-STYLE WHOLEMEAL
- ☐ HIGH-GLUTEN
- ☐ HIGH-EXTRACTION
  - ___ *Type 70 malted*
  - ___ *Stone ground type 80*
  - ___ *Type 80*
  - ___ *Old country type 85*
  - ___ *Old country type 85 malted*
- ☐ OTHER _____

- ☐ SPECIALTY
  - ___ *Barley*
  - ___ *Coarse cornmeal*
  - ___ *Fine cornmeal*
  - ___ *Polenta*
  - ___ *Flaxseed meal*
  - ___ *Millet*
  - ___ *Brown rice*
  - ___ *White rice*
  - ___ *Cream of rye*
  - ___ *Pumpernickel rye*
  - ___ *White rye*
  - ___ *Whole dark rye*
  - ___ *Spelt*
  - ___ *Semolina*
  - ___ *Whole durum*
  - ___ *Whole-wheat durum*

TYPES OF SALT

- ☐ IODIZED TABLE SALT
- ☐ KOSHER MEDIUM-COARSE SALT
- ☐ PINK HIMALAYAN SALT
- ☐ VOLCANIC BLACK SALT
- ☐ MALDON SALT
- ☐ EXTRA FINE SEA SALT
- ☐ FRENCH GRAY SEA SALT
- ☐ SMOKED SEA SALT
- ☐ SEL GRIS

BAKING CONDITIONS

HUMIDITY

TEMPERATURE

STARTER DESCRIPTION

FINISHED LOAF DESCRIPTION

CRUMB DESCRIPTORS

- ☐ EVEN, "TIGHT" HOLES
- ☐ EVEN, MEDIUM HOLES
- ☐ IRREGULAR, LARGE HOLES
- ☐ DELICATE STRUCTURE
- ☐ AVERAGE STRUCTURE
- ☐ STURDY STRUCTURE
- ☐ TRANSLUCENT
- ☐ DENSE
- ☐ COOL AND CREAMY
- ☐ DRY OR DUSTY
- ☐ OTHER _____

CRUST DESCRIPTORS

- ☐ TENDER, GOLDEN
- ☐ SOFT, COMPRESSIBLE
- ☐ HARD, CRUSTY
- ☐ CARAMELIZED
- ☐ NUTTY
- ☐ BUTTERY
- ☐ OILY
- ☐ TOOTHSOME
- ☐ CRISPY
- ☐ OTHER _____

DATE _____

NOTES

INGREDIENTS

TYPES OF FLOUR

- ☐ ALL-PURPOSE
- ☐ UNBLEACHED ALL-PURPOSE
- ☐ BREAD FLOUR
- ☐ UNBLEACHED WHEAT
  - ___ *Plus malted*
  - ___ *Low ash*
  - ___ *Malted All-purpose*
  - ___ *High-gluten*
- ☐ WHOLE-WHEAT
  - ___ *Fine*
  - ___ *High-protein fine*
  - ___ *Medium*
  - ___ *High-protein medium*
  - ___ *Coarse*
  - ___ *High-protein coarse*
  - ___ *Special medium/coarse*

- ☐ HARD WHITE WHOLE-WHEAT
- ☐ BROMATED HIGH-PROTEIN
- ☐ UNBLEACHED ENRICHED
- ☐ BLEACHED WHEAT
- ☐ ARTISAN BREAD
- ☐ IRISH-STYLE WHOLEMEAL
- ☐ HIGH-GLUTEN
- ☐ HIGH-EXTRACTION
  - ___ *Type 70 malted*
  - ___ *Stone ground type 80*
  - ___ *Type 80*
  - ___ *Old country type 85*
  - ___ *Old country type 85 malted*
- ☐ OTHER _____

- ☐ SPECIALTY
  - ___ *Barley*
  - ___ *Coarse cornmeal*
  - ___ *Fine cornmeal*
  - ___ *Polenta*
  - ___ *Flaxseed meal*
  - ___ *Millet*
  - ___ *Brown rice*
  - ___ *White rice*
  - ___ *Cream of rye*
  - ___ *Pumpernickel rye*
  - ___ *White rye*
  - ___ *Whole dark rye*
  - ___ *Spelt*
  - ___ *Semolina*
  - ___ *Whole durum*
  - ___ *Whole-wheat durum*

TYPES OF SALT

- ☐ IODIZED TABLE SALT
- ☐ KOSHER MEDIUM-COARSE SALT
- ☐ PINK HIMALAYAN SALT
- ☐ VOLCANIC BLACK SALT
- ☐ MALDON SALT
- ☐ EXTRA FINE SEA SALT
- ☐ FRENCH GRAY SEA SALT
- ☐ SMOKED SEA SALT
- ☐ SEL GRIS

BAKING CONDITIONS

HUMIDITY

TEMPERATURE

STARTER DESCRIPTION

FINISHED LOAF DESCRIPTION

CRUMB DESCRIPTORS

- ☐ EVEN, "TIGHT" HOLES
- ☐ EVEN, MEDIUM HOLES
- ☐ IRREGULAR, LARGE HOLES
- ☐ DELICATE STRUCTURE
- ☐ AVERAGE STRUCTURE
- ☐ STURDY STRUCTURE
- ☐ TRANSLUCENT
- ☐ DENSE
- ☐ COOL AND CREAMY
- ☐ DRY OR DUSTY
- ☐ OTHER _____

CRUST DESCRIPTORS

- ☐ TENDER, GOLDEN
- ☐ SOFT, COMPRESSIBLE
- ☐ HARD, CRUSTY
- ☐ CARAMELIZED
- ☐ NUTTY
- ☐ BUTTERY
- ☐ OILY
- ☐ TOOTHSOME
- ☐ CRISPY
- ☐ OTHER _____

DATE _____

NOTES

INGREDIENTS

- ☐ ALL-PURPOSE
- ☐ UNBLEACHED ALL-PURPOSE
- ☐ BREAD FLOUR
- ☐ UNBLEACHED WHEAT
  - ___ *Plus malted*
  - ___ *Low ash*
  - ___ *Malted All-purpose*
  - ___ *High-gluten*
- ☐ WHOLE-WHEAT
  - ___ *Fine*
  - ___ *High protein fine*
  - ___ *Medium*
  - ___ *High-protein medium*
  - ___ *Coarse*
  - ___ *High-protein coarse*
  - ___ *Special medium/coarse*

- ☐ HARD WHITE WHOLE-WHEAT
- ☐ BROMATED HIGH-PROTEIN
- ☐ UNBLEACHED ENRICHED
- ☐ BLEACHED WHEAT
- ☐ ARTISAN BREAD
- ☐ IRISH-STYLE WHOLEMEAL
- ☐ HIGH-GLUTEN
- ☐ HIGH-EXTRACTION
  - ___ *Type 70 malted*
  - ___ *Stone ground type 80*
  - ___ *Type 80*
  - ___ *Old country type 85*
  - ___ *Old country type 85 malted*
- ☐ OTHER _____

- ☐ SPECIALTY
  - ___ *Barley*
  - ___ *Coarse cornmeal*
  - ___ *Fine cornmeal*
  - ___ *Polenta*
  - ___ *Flaxseed meal*
  - ___ *Millet*
  - ___ *Brown rice*
  - ___ *White rice*
  - ___ *Cream of rye*
  - ___ *Pumpernickel rye*
  - ___ *White rye*
  - ___ *Whole dark rye*
  - ___ *Spelt*
  - ___ *Semolina*
  - ___ *Whole durum*
  - ___ *Whole-wheat durum*

TYPES OF SALT

- ☐ IODIZED TABLE SALT
- ☐ KOSHER MEDIUM-COARSE SALT
- ☐ PINK HIMALAYAN SALT
- ☐ VOLCANIC BLACK SALT
- ☐ MALDON SALT
- ☐ EXTRA FINE SEA SALT
- ☐ FRENCH GRAY SEA SALT
- ☐ SMOKED SEA SALT
- ☐ SEL GRIS

BAKING CONDITIONS

HUMIDITY

TEMPERATURE

STARTER DESCRIPTION

FINISHED LOAF DESCRIPTION

CRUMB DESCRIPTORS

- ☐ EVEN, "TIGHT" HOLES
- ☐ EVEN, MEDIUM HOLES
- ☐ IRREGULAR, LARGE HOLES
- ☐ DELICATE STRUCTURE
- ☐ AVERAGE STRUCTURE
- ☐ STURDY STRUCTURE
- ☐ TRANSLUCENT
- ☐ DENSE
- ☐ COOL AND CREAMY
- ☐ DRY OR DUSTY
- ☐ OTHER

CRUST DESCRIPTORS

- ☐ TENDER, GOLDEN
- ☐ SOFT, COMPRESSIBLE
- ☐ HARD, CRUSTY
- ☐ CARAMELIZED
- ☐ NUTTY
- ☐ BUTTERY
- ☐ OILY
- ☐ TOOTHSOME
- ☐ CRISPY
- ☐ OTHER _____

DATE _____

NOTES

INGREDIENTS

TYPES OF FLOUR

- ☐ ALL-PURPOSE
- ☐ UNBLEACHED ALL-PURPOSE
- ☐ BREAD FLOUR
- ☐ UNBLEACHED WHEAT
  - ___ *Plus malted*
  - ___ *Low ash*
  - ___ *Malted All-purpose*
  - ___ *High-gluten*
- ☐ WHOLE-WHEAT
  - ___ *Fine*
  - ___ *High-protein fine*
  - ___ *Medium*
  - ___ *High-protein medium*
  - ___ *Coarse*
  - ___ *High-protein coarse*
  - ___ *Special medium/coarse*

- ☐ HARD WHITE WHOLE-WHEAT
- ☐ BROMATED HIGH-PROTEIN
- ☐ UNBLEACHED ENRICHED
- ☐ BLEACHED WHEAT
- ☐ ARTISAN BREAD
- ☐ IRISH-STYLE WHOLEMEAL
- ☐ HIGH-GLUTEN
- ☐ HIGH-EXTRACTION
  - ___ *Type 70 malted*
  - ___ *Stone ground type 80*
  - ___ *Type 80*
  - ___ *Old country type 85*
  - ___ *Old country type 85 malted*
- ☐ OTHER _____

- ☐ SPECIALTY
  - ___ *Barley*
  - ___ *Coarse cornmeal*
  - ___ *Fine cornmeal*
  - ___ *Polenta*
  - ___ *Flaxseed meal*
  - ___ *Millet*
  - ___ *Brown rice*
  - ___ *White rice*
  - ___ *Cream of rye*
  - ___ *Pumpernickel rye*
  - ___ *White rye*
  - ___ *Whole dark rye*
  - ___ *Spelt*
  - ___ *Semolina*
  - ___ *Whole durum*
  - ___ *Whole-wheat durum*

TYPES OF SALT

- ☐ IODIZED TABLE SALT
- ☐ KOSHER MEDIUM-COARSE SALT
- ☐ PINK HIMALAYAN SALT
- ☐ VOLCANIC BLACK SALT
- ☐ MALDON SALT
- ☐ EXTRA FINE SEA SALT
- ☐ FRENCH GRAY SEA SALT
- ☐ SMOKED SEA SALT
- ☐ SEL GRIS

BAKING CONDITIONS

HUMIDITY

TEMPERATURE

STARTER DESCRIPTION

FINISHED LOAF DESCRIPTION

CRUMB DESCRIPTORS

- ☐ EVEN, "TIGHT" HOLES
- ☐ EVEN, MEDIUM HOLES
- ☐ IRREGULAR, LARGE HOLES
- ☐ DELICATE STRUCTURE
- ☐ AVERAGE STRUCTURE
- ☐ STURDY STRUCTURE
- ☐ TRANSLUCENT
- ☐ DENSE
- ☐ COOL AND CREAMY
- ☐ DRY OR DUSTY
- ☐ OTHER _____

CRUST DESCRIPTORS

- ☐ TENDER, GOLDEN
- ☐ SOFT, COMPRESSIBLE
- ☐ HARD, CRUSTY
- ☐ CARAMELIZED
- ☐ NUTTY
- ☐ BUTTERY
- ☐ OILY
- ☐ TOOTHSOME
- ☐ CRISPY
- ☐ OTHER _____

DATE _____

NOTES

INGREDIENTS

TYPES OF FLOUR

- ☐ ALL-PURPOSE
- ☐ UNBLEACHED ALL-PURPOSE
- ☐ BREAD FLOUR
- ☐ UNBLEACHED WHEAT
  - ___ *Plus malted*
  - ___ *Low ash*
  - ___ *Malted All-purpose*
  - ___ *High-gluten*
- ☐ WHOLE-WHEAT
  - ___ *Fine*
  - ___ *High-protein fine*
  - ___ *Medium*
  - ___ *High-protein medium*
  - ___ *Coarse*
  - ___ *High-protein coarse*
  - ___ *Special medium/coarse*

- ☐ HARD WHITE WHOLE-WHEAT
- ☐ BROMATED HIGH-PROTEIN
- ☐ UNBLEACHED ENRICHED
- ☐ BLEACHED WHEAT
- ☐ ARTISAN BREAD
- ☐ IRISH-STYLE WHOLEMEAL
- ☐ HIGH-GLUTEN
- ☐ HIGH-EXTRACTION
  - ___ *Type 70 malted*
  - ___ *Stone ground type 80*
  - ___ *Type 80*
  - ___ *Old country type 85*
  - ___ *Old country type 85 malted*
- ☐ OTHER _____

- ☐ SPECIALTY
  - ___ *Barley*
  - ___ *Coarse cornmeal*
  - ___ *Fine cornmeal*
  - ___ *Polenta*
  - ___ *Flaxseed meal*
  - ___ *Millet*
  - ___ *Brown rice*
  - ___ *White rice*
  - ___ *Cream of rye*
  - ___ *Pumpernickel rye*
  - ___ *White rye*
  - ___ *Whole dark rye*
  - ___ *Spelt*
  - ___ *Semolina*
  - ___ *Whole durum*
  - ___ *Whole-wheat durum*

TYPES OF SALT

- ☐ IODIZED TABLE SALT
- ☐ KOSHER MEDIUM-COARSE SALT
- ☐ PINK HIMALAYAN SALT
- ☐ VOLCANIC BLACK SALT
- ☐ MALDON SALT
- ☐ EXTRA FINE SEA SALT
- ☐ FRENCH GRAY SEA SALT
- ☐ SMOKED SEA SALT
- ☐ SEL GRIS

BAKING CONDITIONS

HUMIDITY

TEMPERATURE

STARTER DESCRIPTION

FINISHED LOAF DESCRIPTION

CRUMB DESCRIPTORS

- ☐ EVEN, "TIGHT" HOLES
- ☐ EVEN, MEDIUM HOLES
- ☐ IRREGULAR, LARGE HOLES
- ☐ DELICATE STRUCTURE
- ☐ AVERAGE STRUCTURE
- ☐ STURDY STRUCTURE
- ☐ TRANSLUCENT
- ☐ DENSE
- ☐ COOL AND CREAMY
- ☐ DRY OR DUSTY
- ☐ OTHER _____

CRUST DESCRIPTORS

- ☐ TENDER, GOLDEN
- ☐ SOFT, COMPRESSIBLE
- ☐ HARD, CRUSTY
- ☐ CARAMELIZED
- ☐ NUTTY
- ☐ BUTTERY
- ☐ OILY
- ☐ TOOTHSOME
- ☐ CRISPY
- ☐ OTHER _____

DATE _____

TYPES OF FLOUR

- ☐ ALL-PURPOSE
- ☐ UNBLEACHED ALL-PURPOSE
- ☐ BREAD FLOUR
- ☐ UNBLEACHED WHEAT
  - ___ *Plus malted*
  - ___ *Low ash*
  - ___ *Malted All-purpose*
  - ___ *High-gluten*
- ☐ WHOLE-WHEAT
  - ___ *Fine*
  - ___ *High-protein fine*
  - ___ *Medium*
  - ___ *High-protein medium*
  - ___ *Coarse*
  - ___ *High-protein coarse*
  - ___ *Special medium/coarse*

- ☐ HARD WHITE WHOLE-WHEAT
- ☐ BROMATED HIGH-PROTEIN
- ☐ UNBLEACHED ENRICHED
- ☐ BLEACHED WHEAT
- ☐ ARTISAN BREAD
- ☐ IRISH-STYLE WHOLEMEAL
- ☐ HIGH-GLUTEN
- ☐ HIGH-EXTRACTION
  - ___ *Type 70 malted*
  - ___ *Stone ground type 80*
  - ___ *Type 80*
  - ___ *Old country type 85*
  - ___ *Old country type 85 malted*
- ☐ OTHER _____

- ☐ SPECIALTY
  - ___ *Barley*
  - ___ *Coarse cornmeal*
  - ___ *Fine cornmeal*
  - ___ *Polenta*
  - ___ *Flaxseed meal*
  - ___ *Millet*
  - ___ *Brown rice*
  - ___ *White rice*
  - ___ *Cream of rye*
  - ___ *Pumpernickel rye*
  - ___ *White rye*
  - ___ *Whole dark rye*
  - ___ *Spelt*
  - ___ *Semolina*
  - ___ *Whole durum*
  - ___ *Whole-wheat durum*

TYPES OF SALT

- ☐ IODIZED TABLE SALT
- ☐ KOSHER MEDIUM-COARSE SALT
- ☐ PINK HIMALAYAN SALT
- ☐ VOLCANIC BLACK SALT
- ☐ MALDON SALT
- ☐ EXTRA FINE SEA SALT
- ☐ FRENCH GRAY SEA SALT
- ☐ SMOKED SEA SALT
- ☐ SEL GRIS

BAKING CONDITIONS

HUMIDITY

TEMPERATURE

STARTER DESCRIPTION

FINISHED LOAF DESCRIPTION

CRUMB DESCRIPTORS

- ☐ EVEN, "TIGHT" HOLES
- ☐ EVEN, MEDIUM HOLES
- ☐ IRREGULAR, LARGE HOLES
- ☐ DELICATE STRUCTURE
- ☐ AVERAGE STRUCTURE
- ☐ STURDY STRUCTURE
- ☐ TRANSLUCENT
- ☐ DENSE
- ☐ COOL AND CREAMY
- ☐ DRY OR DUSTY
- ☐ OTHER _____

CRUST DESCRIPTORS

- ☐ TENDER, GOLDEN
- ☐ SOFT, COMPRESSIBLE
- ☐ HARD, CRUSTY
- ☐ CARAMELIZED
- ☐ NUTTY
- ☐ BUTTERY
- ☐ OILY
- ☐ TOOTHSOME
- ☐ CRISPY
- ☐ OTHER _____

DATE _____

INGREDIENTS

TYPES OF FLOUR

- ☐ ALL-PURPOSE
- ☐ UNBLEACHED ALL-PURPOSE
- ☐ BREAD FLOUR
- ☐ UNBLEACHED WHEAT
  - ___ *Plus malted*
  - ___ *Low ash*
  - ___ *Malted All-purpose*
  - ___ *High-gluten*
- ☐ WHOLE-WHEAT
  - ___ *Fine*
  - ___ *High- protein fine*
  - ___ *Medium*
  - ___ *High-protein medium*
  - ___ *Coarse*
  - ___ *High-protein coarse*
  - ___ *Special medium/coarse*

- ☐ HARD WHITE WHOLE-WHEAT
- ☐ BROMATED HIGH-PROTEIN
- ☐ UNBLEACHED ENRICHED
- ☐ BLEACHED WHEAT
- ☐ ARTISAN BREAD
- ☐ IRISH-STYLE WHOLEMEAL
- ☐ HIGH-GLUTEN
- ☐ HIGH-EXTRACTION
  - ___ *Type 70 malted*
  - ___ *Stone ground type 80*
  - ___ *Type 80*
  - ___ *Old country type 85*
  - ___ *Old country type 85 malted*
- ☐ OTHER _____

- ☐ SPECIALTY
  - ___ *Barley*
  - ___ *Coarse cornmeal*
  - ___ *Fine cornmeal*
  - ___ *Polenta*
  - ___ *Flaxseed meal*
  - ___ *Millet*
  - ___ *Brown rice*
  - ___ *White rice*
  - ___ *Cream of rye*
  - ___ *Pumpernickel rye*
  - ___ *White rye*
  - ___ *Whole dark rye*
  - ___ *Spelt*
  - ___ *Semolina*
  - ___ *Whole durum*
  - ___ *Whole-wheat durum*

TYPES OF SALT

- ☐ IODIZED TABLE SALT
- ☐ KOSHER MEDIUM-COARSE SALT
- ☐ PINK HIMALAYAN SALT
- ☐ VOLCANIC BLACK SALT
- ☐ MALDON SALT
- ☐ EXTRA FINE SEA SALT
- ☐ FRENCH GRAY SEA SALT
- ☐ SMOKED SEA SALT
- ☐ SEL GRIS

BAKING CONDITIONS

HUMIDITY

TEMPERATURE

STARTER DESCRIPTION

FINISHED LOAF DESCRIPTION

CRUMB DESCRIPTORS

- ☐ EVEN, "TIGHT" HOLES
- ☐ EVEN, MEDIUM HOLES
- ☐ IRREGULAR, LARGE HOLES
- ☐ DELICATE STRUCTURE
- ☐ AVERAGE STRUCTURE
- ☐ STURDY STRUCTURE
- ☐ TRANSLUCENT
- ☐ DENSE
- ☐ COOL AND CREAMY
- ☐ DRY OR DUSTY
- ☐ OTHER _____

CRUST DESCRIPTORS

- ☐ TENDER, GOLDEN
- ☐ SOFT, COMPRESSIBLE
- ☐ HARD, CRUSTY
- ☐ CARAMELIZED
- ☐ NUTTY
- ☐ BUTTERY
- ☐ OILY
- ☐ TOOTHSOME
- ☐ CRISPY
- ☐ OTHER _____

DATE _____

INGREDIENTS

TYPES OF FLOUR

- ☐ ALL-PURPOSE
- ☐ UNBLEACHED ALL-PURPOSE
- ☐ BREAD FLOUR
- ☐ UNBLEACHED WHEAT
  - ___ *Plus malted*
  - ___ *Low ash*
  - ___ *Malted All-purpose*
  - ___ *High-gluten*
- ☐ WHOLE-WHEAT
  - ___ *Fine*
  - ___ *High-protein fine*
  - ___ *Medium*
  - ___ *High-protein medium*
  - ___ *Coarse*
  - ___ *High-protein coarse*
  - ___ *Special medium/coarse*

- ☐ HARD WHITE WHOLE-WHEAT
- ☐ BROMATED HIGH-PROTEIN
- ☐ UNBLEACHED ENRICHED
- ☐ BLEACHED WHEAT
- ☐ ARTISAN BREAD
- ☐ IRISH-STYLE WHOLEMEAL
- ☐ HIGH-GLUTEN
- ☐ HIGH-EXTRACTION
  - ___ *Type 70 malted*
  - ___ *Stone ground type 80*
  - ___ *Type 80*
  - ___ *Old country type 85*
  - ___ *Old country type 85 malted*
- ☐ OTHER _____

- ☐ SPECIALTY
  - ___ *Barley*
  - ___ *Coarse cornmeal*
  - ___ *Fine cornmeal*
  - ___ *Polenta*
  - ___ *Flaxseed meal*
  - ___ *Millet*
  - ___ *Brown rice*
  - ___ *White rice*
  - ___ *Cream of rye*
  - ___ *Pumpernickel rye*
  - ___ *White rye*
  - ___ *Whole dark rye*
  - ___ *Spelt*
  - ___ *Semolina*
  - ___ *Whole durum*
  - ___ *Whole-wheat durum*

TYPES OF SALT

- ☐ IODIZED TABLE SALT
- ☐ KOSHER MEDIUM-COARSE SALT
- ☐ PINK HIMALAYAN SALT
- ☐ VOLCANIC BLACK SALT
- ☐ MALDON SALT
- ☐ EXTRA FINE SEA SALT
- ☐ FRENCH GRAY SEA SALT
- ☐ SMOKED SEA SALT
- ☐ SEL GRIS

BAKING CONDITIONS

HUMIDITY

TEMPERATURE

STARTER DESCRIPTION

FINISHED LOAF DESCRIPTION

CRUMB DESCRIPTORS

- ☐ EVEN, "TIGHT" HOLES
- ☐ EVEN, MEDIUM HOLES
- ☐ IRREGULAR, LARGE HOLES
- ☐ DELICATE STRUCTURE
- ☐ AVERAGE STRUCTURE
- ☐ STURDY STRUCTURE
- ☐ TRANSLUCENT
- ☐ DENSE
- ☐ COOL AND CREAMY
- ☐ DRY OR DUSTY
- ☐ OTHER _____

CRUST DESCRIPTORS

- ☐ TENDER, GOLDEN
- ☐ SOFT, COMPRESSIBLE
- ☐ HARD, CRUSTY
- ☐ CARAMELIZED
- ☐ NUTTY
- ☐ BUTTERY
- ☐ OILY
- ☐ TOOTHSOME
- ☐ CRISPY
- ☐ OTHER _____

DATE _____

NOTES

INGREDIENTS

TYPES OF FLOUR

- ☐ ALL-PURPOSE
- ☐ UNBLEACHED ALL-PURPOSE
- ☐ BREAD FLOUR
- ☐ UNBLEACHED WHEAT
  - ___ *Plus malted*
  - ___ *Low ash*
  - ___ *Malted All-purpose*
  - ___ *High-gluten*
- ☐ WHOLE-WHEAT
  - ___ *Fine*
  - ___ *High-protein fine*
  - ___ *Medium*
  - ___ *High-protein medium*
  - ___ *Coarse*
  - ___ *High-protein coarse*
  - ___ *Special medium/coarse*

- ☐ HARD WHITE WHOLE-WHEAT
- ☐ BROMATED HIGH-PROTEIN
- ☐ UNBLEACHED ENRICHED
- ☐ BLEACHED WHEAT
- ☐ ARTISAN BREAD
- ☐ IRISH-STYLE WHOLEMEAL
- ☐ HIGH-GLUTEN
- ☐ HIGH-EXTRACTION
  - ___ *Type 70 malted*
  - ___ *Stone ground type 80*
  - ___ *Type 80*
  - ___ *Old country type 85*
  - ___ *Old country type 85 malted*
- ☐ OTHER _____

- ☐ SPECIALTY
  - ___ *Barley*
  - ___ *Coarse cornmeal*
  - ___ *Fine cornmeal*
  - ___ *Polenta*
  - ___ *Flaxseed meal*
  - ___ *Millet*
  - ___ *Brown rice*
  - ___ *White rice*
  - ___ *Cream of rye*
  - ___ *Pumpernickel rye*
  - ___ *White rye*
  - ___ *Whole dark rye*
  - ___ *Spelt*
  - ___ *Semolina*
  - ___ *Whole durum*
  - ___ *Whole-wheat durum*

TYPES OF SALT

- ☐ IODIZED TABLE SALT
- ☐ KOSHER MEDIUM-COARSE SALT
- ☐ PINK HIMALAYAN SALT
- ☐ VOLCANIC BLACK SALT
- ☐ MALDON SALT
- ☐ EXTRA FINE SEA SALT
- ☐ FRENCH GRAY SEA SALT
- ☐ SMOKED SEA SALT
- ☐ SEL GRIS

BAKING CONDITIONS

HUMIDITY

TEMPERATURE

STARTER DESCRIPTION

FINISHED LOAF DESCRIPTION

CRUMB DESCRIPTORS

- ☐ EVEN, "TIGHT" HOLES
- ☐ EVEN, MEDIUM HOLES
- ☐ IRREGULAR, LARGE HOLES
- ☐ DELICATE STRUCTURE
- ☐ AVERAGE STRUCTURE
- ☐ STURDY STRUCTURE
- ☐ TRANSLUCENT
- ☐ DENSE
- ☐ COOL AND CREAMY
- ☐ DRY OR DUSTY
- ☐ OTHER _____

CRUST DESCRIPTORS

- ☐ TENDER, GOLDEN
- ☐ SOFT, COMPRESSIBLE
- ☐ HARD, CRUSTY
- ☐ CARAMELIZED
- ☐ NUTTY
- ☐ BUTTERY
- ☐ OILY
- ☐ TOOTHSOME
- ☐ CRISPY
- ☐ OTHER _____

DATE _____

NOTES